Real Animal Communication Stories No. 7
by
'The Animal Psychic'

Jackie Weaver

Other books by the author:
Animal Insight
Animal Talking Tales
Celebrity Pet Talking
The Voice of Spirit Animals
Animal Communication from Heaven and Earth
For the Love of Pets

Jackie Weaver © Copyright 2016

All rights reserved

www.animalpsychic.co.uk

ISBN 978-1540640086

5st December 2016

No parts of this publication may be reproduced, stored in a retrieval system, or transmitted in any form or by any means, electronic, mechanical, photocopying, recording or otherwise without the prior permission of the publisher.

Cover Image by Personaldesigns © Copyright 2016

All rights reserved

I would like to thank all the amazing people I know who continue to support me on this wondrous journey.

I give my heartfelt thanks to all the animals I communicate with and their owners for sharing their stories too.

Thanks to all of these animals for their love, wisdom, and giving proof that they can communicate with us humans is truly incredible – I am truly honoured to do the work I do. To be able to connect with them from Heaven also, I think in itself is miraculous and the words within these pages hopefully will describe the joy and peace that can bring.

ITV This Morning September 2016

(The 3rd anniversary of Stan's passing, so how fitting that was.)

Real Animal Communication Stories No.7

Introduction	7
Lilly and her dog Panda	11
Maria and Molly the dog	21
Valerie and her horse Jet	24
Joanne and her dog Casper	33
Moyra and her cat Ali	37
Rebecca and her cat Nefertiti and Co!	44
Donna and her horse Blue	50
Mel and her dog Ozzie	55
Suzanne and her hawk Nariel	60
Sema and her dog Smiley	64
Eleanor and her dog TJ	69
Letting Go	78
Rosemary and her dog Jasper	81
Sara and her horse Milly	85
Michelle and her dog Ziggy	90
Lesley and her cat Sox	97

Rachael and her dog Frank	107
Holly and her pony Jimmy	112
Chrissie and her dog Chance	121
Debbie and her dog Freddie	129
Kate and Paul's cat Oscar	135
Anne and her dog Emma	139
Postscript	145

Introduction

Hello and welcome to my seventh book! As I write 'seventh book', I too am astounded as I was not exactly academic at school, I was far more an animal person then too. I would have rather been outside on the farm digging up pet worms for my pet hen 'Clucky' or jumping on a pony and seeing where we landed up.

Amazingly, for someone who has 'come from nowhere to somewhere' as I see myself, I have actually have more books published that any other UK animal communicator! I really struggled to think of yet another title (or even to remember those of former books) so I decided, that I would make things easier for you the readers, and me the writer, to simply number them from now on. I will still indulge in my photography and try to give you my personal covers. This one is of Chico, my Jack Russell who has truly learnt how to pose for me. Bless him, from a rescue dog I got at six months, who had never even been out on a walk (!) he is living the life of Riley and learning the rules, just about!

It is now 2016 and I am now 10 years past my 'terminal' cancer and whilst people often moan about birthdays over a certain half way mark, I celebrate mine with thanks as I truly have beaten the odds. Any wrinkles I can blame on chemotherapy or laughing and talking too much – the latter is far more me as my life is full of chatter and fun.

These odds are not just my illness, but my whole life... People imagine because I get asked to go on television and radio shows (this year I have been on ITV Loose Women and also ITV This Morning again) that my life must be so easy, and that I am so blessed. Well, blessed it is for the work I do, but life has been far from easy at times. I am so very lucky that through spirit, I have met some wonderful people who have helped me, taught me so much and I know that even the things that go wrong are simply lessons for us to learn from. I have also learnt, that I can't please everyone, nobody can. I live spiritually and believe that as long I do the best that I can, and for the right reasons, then I am at peace with myself.

Every reading is different and there are many varying factors – some animals are clearer and more chatty than others – this selection is where animals have given information with such clarity and even bits I was staggered by and I was doing the readings!

I have taken the biggest lesson of all from animals, needless to say, and discovering that living for the day *is* the way to live. How often have you been shocked when something so unexpected happened? The times when all your best-laid plans took a complete U-turn, you realized further down the line, that actually it was for the best? Animals get up in the morning with the expectations of another day and live it as it comes – I really try to do the same well, as best as I can.

My work is a dream come true… to be able to help ease animal owners' pain and solve problems is immeasurable. I have to say though, that not all readings are easy and I, like other people who do the same job, have to get past my logical brain and be brave – yes brave! I take my work very seriously (although have many good laughs doing it) and could you imagine simply connecting with an animal, who lives anywhere, even in spirit and giving credible information to their owner? Well, that is what I try to do on a daily basis and am grateful that somehow I can. I never take it for granted. If I had a £1 for every time I thank spirit and my wonderful guides, especially darling Stan who came into my life to leave and then help me as a spirit guide, I wouldn't really need to sell any books!

Once again, wonderful and loving owners have shared their own true accounts of our communications, in their own words, and I have added a few stories of my own that I had written previously and would like to share.

I hope that this book helps you if you are grieving for a passed over animal or even a person. After all, we all go to the same place and are re-united. Or you may find it helps to just to realise that animals truly do understand what we say, so maybe you will try explaining things clearly to your animal and see if it makes a difference if needed to try and solve something. Animals, like children, need to know their boundaries and once they do, they often are happier knowing what is acceptable and, what is not.

I do declare that you may need some tissues when reading these stories but also that you may even laugh out loud too. Animals really do have a fantastic sense of humour and I hope you enjoy my book number seven.

My darling Sally, who I love so very much.

She is now nearly twelve-years-old and the most amazing and wonderful soul who has also helped teach so many people how to communicate with animals. She is the perfect example of how some animals, in spite of having a terrible start to life, can learn to trust and be happy once again and make such a difference to so many other people's lives.

Real Animal Communication Stories No.7

He changed their lives forever...

Lily and her dog Panda

Panda was the most incredibly wonderful dog I could ever imagine having the privilege to know. He came into our lives in March 2014. My husband and I had decided that we wanted to adopt a rescue dog as a companion for our Cavalier, Tails. He was two at the time and we felt we would like to have another canine friend in the household.

We were concerned that we wouldn't be allowed a rescue dog because we live in a flat without a garden and had seen on quite a few shelter websites that a garden was a requirement. With some trepidation, I emailed a shelter in Wales to ask whether they would consider potential adopters without a garden. I was very fortunate to receive a reply from the shelter's owner explaining that many of their dogs came from puppy farms and would need a garden, but that they had just rescued a King Charles Cavalier from Ireland, who she thought would be suitable. He was aged about four to six-years-old and his previous guardian had died, but as the relatives didn't want him, he was taken to the pound. (Sadly, In Ireland, abandoned dogs are routinely euthanised within twenty-four hours of arriving, but this Cavalier had been rescued in the nick of time and brought to the shelter in Wales.) As soon as his profile was uploaded to the website, we put in an application and were delighted when it was accepted. Only a few days later we were bringing him home with us!

The rescuers hadn't known his name and were calling him Paul, but we decided to name him Panda – not only because he was black and white (with only the tiniest bit of brown, including his eyebrows!), but also because he was round and chunky, and the way he walked reminded us of a Panda Bear. When Panda first came to us, he was very anxious and defensive because of the trauma that he had been through, but nevertheless, we were amazed how gentle and loving he was from the day he first met us. He had clearly been through a period of neglect before his rescue, as when we adopted him he was deaf from a long-term ear infection and had to have seven rotten teeth removed. Despite how much he must have been suffering he always remained good-natured. It was delightful to see how his hearing came back when the ear infection was treated and how he started to smile when his teeth had been sorted out.

Over the coming months he revealed himself to be the sweetest and most affectionate dog we could have imagined. He loved to go under the duvet and he would stay there with only his tail sticking out, and he loved to cuddle with us all night. His special brand of greeting was to give us kisses on the nose (no where else, only the nose would do!) and he would also do this to reassure us whenever we were worried about something. We often felt that Panda was more like a furry little person than a dog, and unlike Tails, he wasn't interested in meeting other dogs. He didn't really like the park, and didn't much care when the doorbell rang. He hated mornings (very much like me) and loved nothing more than a nice long lie-in. He was always very sensible and we had the impression that he felt like he didn't need to walk on a lead and harness, and only put up with it to humour us. Sometimes, when we took him and Tails on holiday to North Wales, we would let him walk off lead. He was always delighted with this arrangement and, unlike Tails, who would run off, jump into hedges, and generally cause mischief if given the chance, Panda would walk along sedately and responsibly next to us.

Panda loved nothing more than delicious food and would often keep us company in the kitchen when we were cooking, so that he could supervise the whole meal preparation process. We often joked that he would make a great chef, except that he would eat all of the ingredients before the food was cooked. When the online grocery deliveries arrived, he would lie next to the boxes and carefully guard them so that Tails couldn't get too close. He amazed us with his ability to use a spoon – he understood what it was for and would eat the food off of it just like a person, instead of licking at it like Tails did. His powers of concentration and problem-solving were legendary when it came to obtaining food: he would often discover a piece of kibble hiding under a bookcase or the sofa, and if he couldn't get it out with his paw he would lie in front of the offending item of furniture making chirping noises until one of us came and got it out for him. Many times we couldn't find it and would think he was mistaken, but he would insist and so we would look further and he always turned out to be right. If one of us left a bowl of food up on a bookshelf (which we had to do because he would unashamedly devour anything left unattended on the table), he would start trying to scale it like a miniature mountain climber, and you could see him carefully plotting out his route, hoping that this time he would make it to the top shelf. Panda had a very strong personality, and as the months went by he started to express his opinions more and more. He would only consent to going to the park in the morning, but in the afternoon he would refuse to go back as he thought that more than one park trip a day was uncivilised! Instead, he preferred exploring the streets of Northwest London, and would often lead us on adventures to shopping centres and housing estates where we had never been before. Being an avowed night-owl, he felt that the final walk of the evening was the perfect time for a nice long stroll.

The first time we took Panda to the vet we were told that he had a low grade heart murmur (which sadly is very common in Cavaliers due to their small gene pool), but that we shouldn't worry, as hopefully it wouldn't progress into heart disease for a long time. When Panda had been with us for a little less than a year he started to cough and was diagnosed with mitral valve disease, which causes congestive heart failure. We were absolutely devastated by the news as we knew that the prognosis for congestive heart failure is not usually very good. Panda was already such a treasured member of our family that the thought of life without him was unimaginably terrifying. The vet was very reassuring, saying that he had known a Cavalier who lived for seven years with the disease, and we hoped that the same would be true for Panda. He was put on medication and managed very well for about a year, only coughing occasionally. We really hoped that he would beat the odds and stay with us for many more years to come.

Tragically, at the end of January 2016, his condition suddenly worsened and we ended up having to rush him to hospital when he had a terrible crisis and was struggling to breathe. He was put on oxygen and given emergency medication to try to empty his lungs of fluid. They told us that his heart condition was now very advanced. They said we should start thinking about euthanasia but that they would try to stabilise him and, with luck, he may be able to come home for another few weeks. We felt like the Earth had been torn from underneath us. At that time all we wanted was for him to be able to come home, and didn't want to think about what would happen afterwards. We were very lucky that Panda stabilised and within a few days was able to come off the oxygen and return home with us. We treasured every moment with him, knowing that each day could be the last. The hospital made us an appointment with a specialist who confirmed the prognosis. He said that he would try switching one of his medications to a last-resort alternative in the hope that he would be able to live to see the beginning of spring. He told us that Panda could have another crisis at any time and that we would just have to monitor him and hope for the best. Our vet mentioned that he knew a dog in a similar position that had beaten the odds and lived two years beyond his expected prognosis so, despite everything, we held out some hope that Panda would make a similar miraculous recovery.

After an initial adjustment period on a new medication, he seemed to be more like his old self and he seemed to become more vigorous and even puppyish: the day before he left us he chased some other dogs around the park, something which he had never ever done before! On the same day the first daffodils appeared in the neighbourhood and we took this as a symbolic indication that he had made it through to the beginning of spring. We took a lot of photos of him standing next to them on our way back from the park. The next evening Panda went into another dreaded crisis and we rushed him to hospital. The vet confirmed that there was nothing else that could be done for him and so we had to make the most agonising decision of our lives and agree for him to be put to sleep. The vet and nurse laid down a blanket and we found some treats to feed Panda.

Though he had pretty much lost his appetite, he was very happy to eat the treats. We were both crying and he gave each of us a lick on the nose to reassure us that he was going to be all right. Somehow we felt that he knew what was about to happen, even though at the same time we were tormented by the awful sensation that we were being forced to make this momentous decision on his behalf and, without his consent. We cuddled him as the vet administered his injection. He kept eating treats for a couple of moments and then stopped as if he had noticed something in the distance, before lying down and drawing his last breath. He looked so peaceful, as if he was just sleeping, but we immediately burst into tears knowing that his spirit had left his body.

We walked home in a cloud of the most unbearable grief either of us had ever known – it was much worse than we had felt at the loss of close human relatives, because we had shared such a special bond with Panda. Over the next few days through the agonising grief we were tormented by thoughts of whether we had indeed made the right decision, even though the vet had made it clear that there were no other options, and couldn't stop wondering what had happened to Panda's soul, asking ourselves whether he was still alive in spirit form. We also both dreamed of him in the days after he left us, and felt like we were receiving other coded messages from him. Not sure whether such a thing was really possible, I started searching the Internet for after-death communication, and was amazed to discover a wealth of online information about exactly the sorts of dreams and signs that we thought we had been receiving. At that point I started to wonder whether it would be possible to find an animal medium who could contact Panda's spirit. Another Google search

Real Animal Communication Stories No.7

led me to Jackie; I read her book which contained numerous stories of detailed communications with the spirits of beloved pets. Reading these testimonials gave me the resolution to book a Skype session, but we were both still sceptical, despite desperately wanting to believe that it was possible to contact Panda. It seemed too good to be true.

When the session came we were both excited and nervous, not sure what to expect. Jackie was so warm and friendly that we were immediately reassured. She told us that she had connected with Panda, and that he had told her that he was a very gentle dog, 'man's best-friend', without an ounce of aggression, and was content to potter around the house and wasn't very exuberant. This did sound like Panda, but it was the next thing she said that really astonished us – she said she had the impression that he hadn't died in an accident, and that he had suffered from an illness that gave him a rattily chest. We were stunned by this accurate detail, since the cough had been the chief symptom of Panda's disease. She then said that she had an image of daffodils in a park, which was equally astounding because the daffodils and the photos we had taken of Panda the day before he passed over were so symbolic and significant to us. This felt like further confirmation that, incredibly, she was really in communication with Panda's spirit, because there was no other way she could have known these specific details.

Jackie went on to say that Panda was with an old lady. We immediately understood that this was his previous guardian who had died in Ireland. Jackie said that the old lady had known Panda was on his way and had been there to welcome him to the spirit world. This was hugely comforting to us, as we had been sick with wondering what had happened to him when his spirit left his body and whether he had to make his way to the 'Other Side' on his own. She made us smile when she said that Panda remembered how we used to have him groomed and would call him a 'handsome boy'. This was another amazingly specific detail, because that was our special name for him, and one that we never called Tails. We both laughed when she told us that she had the impression Panda didn't need a lead to go for a walk – we had always felt that he thought the lead was beneath his dignity! It really felt like Panda's personality was coming through in the conversation, as that seemed like just the sort of thing that he would make a point of telling us if he could.

Something else that astonished us was how Jackie mentioned that Panda used to stop suddenly while out on walks. This was another detail of his life that would be impossible for anyone to guess. Afterwards we told our friends who knew Panda about this, and they were all equally astounded, as it was a peculiarity of his that anyone familiar with him would instantly recognise. Jackie said that it wasn't a physical thing; he was just stopping to take in and admire his new London surroundings. Panda mentioned his past and that he hadn't been a beaten dog, even if his previous life may not always have been fantastic. This was a big comfort to us, as we always worried that Panda may have suffered in his first home before he came to us. We asked what his previous home had been like, and she said she had the impression of a large housing estate, and that Panda said we had now shown him what posh life was like! This made us laugh as well, because we had always had the feeling that he thought something along those lines, and it was so funny to get confirmation of his view.

We asked the question that had been torturing us since the night we lost him, whether it was the right time for him to go. He said that it had been the perfect time, that he knew he wouldn't be on Earth long, and that he had been struggling towards the end. This was extremely reassuring to us, because we had been tormented by the thought that we had made a mistake, and that if he could somehow have been stabilised in hospital we might have had a few more days, or even weeks, with him. He thanked us for taking him in, and for all the love and care we gave him.

He said he had loved being with his previous guardian and then living with us and that it was like 'having the best of both worlds'. He is now back with her, but loves to watch over us here on Earth. We asked what it was like for him in the spirit world, and he said that it was similar to Earth but 'every day is easy', and that he can breathe freely now. This was also hugely reassuring to us, because there was nothing more horrible than having no idea what had happened to him after he left us. We had hoped that he was in a better place, but hadn't dared to dream that his spirit was still completely intact with his memories and personality, just like he was when he was alive, but freed from the terrible suffering caused by his disease. The thought of him enjoying the afterlife with his beloved previous guardian, while watching over us here on Earth, has given us incredible comfort.

Another amazing moment in the session was when Panda told Jackie that I had received an 'unusual letter'. This astounded me because a few days previously I had received a completely unexpected email from my stepsister in California, who I had never met or been in touch with before! She wrote to tell me that she had come into possession of some photos of my father, and other relatives, and she wanted to know if I would like them. Not only that, but only a couple of hours after the Skype session, an envelope arrived with the family photos that she had sent!

During the session Jackie said Panda was giving her the image of a traffic warden and asked if that had any significance for us. We were both puzzled and couldn't imagine what that was about. (Jackie was laughing saying how random it was, but to note it down anyway?) We forgot about it, but a few days later I was missing Panda terribly and asked him please to send us a sign that he was all right. Literally seconds later, a character on the TV show we were watching said something about a traffic warden! I knew at once that this was a sign from Panda, and that he had given Jackie the image so that he could later use it as a message for us.

We still don't understand how this communication works, but have received too many signs like this to be able to write them off as mere coincidences. We can now say without exaggeration that the communication session with Jackie was one of the most meaningful and moving experiences of our lives. Not only did it bring us much-needed peace and comfort that we had thought we would never have again after losing Panda, but it totally changed our beliefs about the afterlife. Before this, we had both been uncertain as to whether there really was such a thing as a spirit world, now we know that it is a truth as undeniable as the existence of oxygen.

While we still miss and cry for Panda's furry earthly presence every day, the knowledge that he is fit and well on the 'Other Side' has been such an indescribable revelation and opened up a whole new universe for us. Now when someone tells us that he is 'in a better place', it doesn't just feel like empty words, as we know it to be true. Since the session we have continued to receive beautiful signs from him, including dream visitations. Although we will always miss his Earthly presence in our lives, the knowledge that he will continue to watch over us and communicate with us until we re-join him in the spirit world, has been the greatest gift imaginable.

*****

With love back to a special lady...

Maria and Mollie the dog.

Unbelievably, I never used to like dogs! For some unknown reason, from being a little girl I was always the one that would cry if a dog came near me. Even as an adult my feelings about them never changed until I was in my 40s, which is why, this is a rather unusual story – even the title for this is not like the others in this book...

I take you back to about eight years ago when I noticed my neighbour had a dog that seemed to spend its time staring at me from a window. I didn't pay that much attention to this dog as my neighbour had had dogs before and they were always barking and, to be honest, that irritated me. I did, however, notice that my cats would sit on the roof to tease this particular dog. The strange thing was, this dog would never bark but just sat there looking at my cats. I don't know why, but one day I felt the urge to offer to take the dog for a walk, so I did! I can only think that the look of this dog's demeanour made me feel sorry for her. Incredibly, my neighbour was happy for me to do so, admitting that she wasn't much of a walker herself.

This was all so new to me; I didn't know how to take one for a walk and learnt by watching others! The dogs name was Mollie and she was a small German Shepherd / Collie cross and was very energetic! Incredibly, I had no fear about Mollie and very soon we developed into a routine of me taking Mollie for a walk several times a week. I was so enchanted by her lovely, happy and sweet demeanour, I realised that I was seeing and walking passed other dogs with no qualms at all! As soon as I arrived at my neighbours, she'd get very excited and we would go out and have such a lovely time. We just went off on our own for hours and hours walking and exploring new places. I was now sharing in the joy of the love and companionship of this very special girl.

Some years later, my neighbour moved a few miles to another village. I was so fond of Mollie, and loved being with her, that there was no way I'd let the house move stops our walks. Fortunately, Mollie's actual owner was pleased with the way this had turned out. She was able to get on with what she did in life knowing that her dog had the best of everything but also fabulous quality time and walks with me. I was kindly given a key and for the next five years I drove to see Mollie a few times a week. As soon as she heard my car, she'd be there at the door waiting for me and off we'd go. She developed a hip problem in the last couple of years of her life, so the big walks weren't quite as long, but that didn't stop my visits. Mollie was such a lovely dog: She never barked, always came back as soon as you called her, and was lovely to other dogs too.

Real Animal Communication Stories No.7

When she was nine years old, she started to have a few fits and the vet suspected she had a tumour in her head. I contacted Jackie to have a reading. Once Jackie was happy with the ethics, as I was not the dog's owner, we had a reading with Mollie. Jackie made it clear she doesn't diagnose (she explains she will pass what the animal gives to her) but did confirm, what I already knew it in my heart, that this was probably an illness that was going to get worse, not better. She gave Jackie a feeling of pressure in her head, which seemed more than the effects of an epileptic dog.

In the reading Mollie actually said, "I always come back when you call" and she did! Always! Mollie confirmed that I was her '2nd mum.' It was important for me that Mollie knew how much I loved her and cared for her. She did. She described a tree we used to play under and said how she thanked me for all the wonderful times we spent together on our wanders.

Sadly, Mollie got progressively worse – she'd have good days and days when she wanted to go out for a walk, but as it can happen with brain tumours, her personality changed a little bit. Some days she didn't want to walk so I'd just sit or lie with her and tell her how much I loved her. I think the medication changed her, as once, whilst walking in a field, for no reason at all, she ran off flat out towards the village. I was terrified I'd lost her and found her just sitting waiting for me at the end of a track. I don't know who was panting more, her or me!

Two days before she passed, she just looked sad and it was obvious she'd had enough. I stroked her ears and kissed her and told her it was okay to go for a big sleep if she wanted. I took her for a walk to her favourite pond and she jumped around smiling and running about like she always did.

The next day I got a text from her owner to say she'd had a very large fit and the time had come. I was at a hospital appointment and couldn't go with her to the vets, but I honestly think Mollie planned it that way. I was very sad but I knew it wasn't right to keep her alive in a poor condition.

I had a reading with Jackie approximately three weeks after Mollie passed. Before the reading I hoped Mollie would mention about me kissing her and stroking her ears – it was the last thing I did with her. When Jackie mentioned this and I got goosebumps and she told me the exact symptoms of Mollie's last day.

The reading was different from what I imagined. I had simply wanted to make sure she was okay (she was) and to know that I still cared for her. However, Mollie wanted me to know that she was grateful for all I did for her and said I was the 'sunshine' in her life. She even told me she was surprised I carried on walking her when they moved. She has visited my house since she passed over and even confirmed I needed to do some dusting! She also suggested it might help me be a little more organised, by writing things on a calendar. I laughed and explained I always intend to, but then get distracted and it doesn't happen. Gosh, I never realised how much she knew about me, amazing. We did have a giggle and Jackie said that spirit animals like to make us smile.

Mollie explained that she was happy with my neighbour but I added the extras! I didn't think this could happen but she changed my life and thanks to her, I learnt the true meaning of unconditional love

Real Animal Communication Stories No.7

from a dog and it was such a joy to be able to share in her life. Jackie told me that Mollie has decided to be my guide in life! I believe it is her way of thanking me for all I did for her. She's decided to be my inspiration and encourage me when I need it. She says now she can be with me anytime, and in my house too! I'm so happy with this. I really do feel her around me a lot and I know we'll always be together. I talk to her all the time. I feel so blessed that Mollie was the dog who turned me into a dog lover and this has changed my life forever.

*****

A lesson for others to learn from…

Valerie and her horse Jet.

Jet was a boisterous but apparently a well-bred pure black colt. He appeared on our yard when he was about eighteen months old. At that time, already having my own veteran gelding, Prince, whom I loved dearly and who had a number of health challenges, I paid very little attention to Jet as he was not my horse so nothing to do with me.

Over the following years I was vaguely aware of Jet being moved to different stables around the yard and the stable door grill following him, along with his "beware this horse bites" sign, until he finally landed in the barn opposite my Prince's stable. Apart from sympathising with people who had been dragged around by Jet, or even bitten by him, I didn't really know what his 'job' was or what he was really like.

Four years later, and as sometimes happens with horses, Prince became less and less comfortable with his conditions until the painful decision was taken to release him from his constant pain. To try to soften the blow of losing Prince the yard owner suggested I try out two of her horses. Now this wasn't to fill a Prince shaped hole, but to give me an opportunity to see if I wanted a part time loan of another horse until I decided what I wanted to do next. The choice was between a lovely thoroughbred that was very popular on the yard and Jet, the black colt that had grown into a rather large boisterous six year old.

I decided to try Jet and seemingly I had tried him on a good day as, in my grief-ridden state, he looked after me rather well. I was aware that during the past four years Jet had had a tumultuous time. I felt a bit sorry for him because, after a couple of years of lots of attention as he was being trained to be an eventing horse, he was subsequently blighted with injury and breathing issues and was no longer considered a viable eventing prospect. He was then kept on months of box rest with a prospect of no job when he recovered. I knew that due to him initially being bought to breed with, he had remained entire until a coming together of issues pointed to it being in both his, and everyone else's, interest to have him gelded. Jet was gelded at six so was already an established stallion with all the behaviours that go with it. Time went on and late in the summer he was turned out and seemed relatively calm. I decided that maybe Jet had had bad press and I wanted to give him a chance and some attention. His owner was happy for me to try with him, and that was eighteen months ago.

We started off quite well, going to fun rides and even local dressage competitions. I have to admit though that I had issues with tacking up, picking out his feet, and generally being around him in the stable where he appeared a little aggressive. We were heading into winter and the clay fields started getting

Real Animal Communication Stories No.7

waterlogged and turn out became an issue. Mud didn't suit Jet and that winter he got cellulitis (fluid retention swellings) in his hind legs. After a few weeks off, we carried on but Jet was more boisterous than ever having been on box-rest – it was like riding a coiled spring and a good job he wasn't a fit horse or he would have been even worse.

He seemed frustrated and he started biting, and quite a lot at that! If you shouted at him, or raised a hand to him to warn him off, (with no intention of hitting him) Jet would come at you with his teeth. If you tried to pick up his feet he would bite or double barrel you depending on which end you were at. I became frightened of going in the stable with him. Beautiful as he was, he was just too big and too strong. Few people on the yard were prepared to handle him, and so on the days I wasn't able to go and see him; he had limited interaction with people at all. Being a former stallion, he had spent his early years in a field with one other gelding so he wasn't properly socialised with other horses and had certainly never been put in his place by another horse.

With spring came turnout and Jet started to calm down a little, but was still bargy and bitey. That summer came more challenges, after I returned from holiday, Jet was ill for three months which meant more box rest and lots of TLC but this amazingly seemed to be a turning point for us. As Jet was feeling under the weather, he was quiet to handle and the constant cleaning and me spending time with him (without the added stress of having to ride him) gave us chance to start to form a bond. We spent hours walking in hand, learning to walk over tarpaulin on the floor and to back out of my space, all the things he wasn't very good at. At this point I saw a glimmer of a different Jet who wanted to be friends.

Just as we were about to get back to ridden work as Jet got better, I broke my leg badly which was nothing to do with Jet. Part of me was relieved that at least I would not have to ride him over winter, but I was frustrated as I thought we had started to make progress.

I was off riding for six months, in the first three months I only saw Jet twice, after that I would talk to him from a few feet away from the outside of his stable door. I was too scared to handle him in case he knocked me over or something happened and I needed to move quickly knowing that due the wet winter and spring was meaning turnout was limited for him yet again.

After first riding a friend's small, calm pony I decided to brave Jet. It was terrible. He would go for me when I tried to tack him up, I'd given up on trying to pick his feet out, he would drag me around after leaping out of his stable then bronc for the first ten minutes of riding him. If a mare was in season on the yard he was quite literally uncontrollable on the end of a lead rope. Me, my confidence, and my leg, couldn't deal with this. Clearly my self-preservation for not hurting my leg was affecting my confidence and now being in a constant state of fear when on or around Jet, was making him jittery too.

Either he had to go back to his owner full time with no job or something had to change.

So, I started thinking about how he must be feeling to behave this way. In my mind, he clearly was not aggressive for the sake of being aggressive and apart from the obvious late gelding, there was something I

Real Animal Communication Stories No.7

just didn't get. I then knew that I couldn't deal with it, or make a decision as to whether or not I was able to deal with it, without some form of intervention.

Years earlier, through Jackie, I had had a chat with Prince on two occasions. I made contact again and explained to Jackie I had lost Prince but I had a new horse that I'd had for eighteen months. At this point I gave nothing away to Jackie of the issues I was having and that this was going to be make or break time for me and Jet.

Friday morning came and Jackie rang, I knew the drill from last time and had sent Jackie Jet's photograph. Jackie had already introduced herself to Jet who had described himself as a big, gregarious but 'riggy' horse! (A rig is a horse with testicles that are undescended so act stallion like.) Nothing to disagree with there! Jet went on to give some clear confirmations such as the cost of his huge vets bill before I had him and some insights into his personality.

Then it started to come out... some kind of horsemanship gone wrong. Someone had tried to take him on with his bullish attitude and made it all worse. Jet acknowledged his threatening behaviour and explained that he had learnt that in the barn he lived in. Someone had taken him on and challenged him very harshly which he had found desperately difficult to deal with. Jet told Jackie he was sorry if he intimidated me but he was trying to protect himself. I was devastated to think Jet saw me as a threat, when in truth it was me scared of him, but I could see that in my panic I could react loudly and make fast gestures which to Jet would come across as threatening. We were clearly totally misunderstanding each other.

We asked Jet why he wouldn't let me pick up his feet. Jet told Jackie that someone had lifted his foot and held it whilst he had been tied up and used this against him in such a way that he was not going to allow that to happen again!

I recalled that someone had come to the yard to train Jet to be an eventer, and over those two years they were the only person who worked with him and rode him too. As this person was 'old school', I can imagine where Jet was coming from. His owner was with this person during these periods and could see what was happening. During our chat it also came out that Jet was holding his owner responsible for letting these things happen. Jackie explained to Jet that she had genuinely believed what she was told and that this more experienced person was doing right with him, and did not understand the implications of what was happening. It took some work for Jackie to reduce the negativity Jet felt for her. (Jet had already admitted that he behaved better for me than her, so this made perfect sense).

Jet went on to talk about being taunted when he was younger, and also people giving up on him. He recognised people did not trust him. He wanted to be trusted but even when he was good people pushed him away. Jackie explained to him that if he could try and trust me and his owner, (as we were both on his side) this would show other people that he could be trusted and thus improve his relationship with everyone he came in contact with.

One of Jet's issues is putting on his bridle. I have to undo the cheek piece, pop the head piece and brow band over his ears, pull the bit through his mouth and refasten the cheek piece. If I try to put the bit on normally he just lifts his head out of reach and bites.

Real Animal Communication Stories No.7

I asked Jackie to ask him why he did this. Jet explained that when he was younger he had been rough handled in a chifney (this is a type of circular control bit that tends to be used on colts and stallions to lead them around) which had bruised his tongue severely due to mishandling. So, in his mind, the pulling up of the bit to get the bridle over his ears in the normal way made him think it was going to hurt him again in the same way as the chifney had.

By now I was in tears and feeling exceptionally guilty that all this time I had misunderstood where he was coming from but the same time I felt I now understood and realised that Jet was not out to get me personally. (I did say at the beginning that maybe he had had bad press and had a feeling that he really was not as he presented himself, and this turned out to be the case.) At the same time I felt I now understood and realised that Jet was not out to get me. Jackie continued to work with Jet after our call had finished and did some release work with him to overcome the trauma he had experienced in the barn.

Jet had also talked about being very mixed up and still feeling entire and hormonal. That his stallion behaviours were still going on so long after he was gelded support these feelings. I am now looking into some type of homeopathic remedy or supplement we can give Jet to help him with this.

I went away for a couple of days after our chat, but got a call from his owner the following day explaining that Jet, having trashed the fence in the field, had got himself tangled up in some wire stock fencing in an area that is usually fenced off. She described him as having his four feet tied together. When the yard girls found him, he was standing totally immobile and trembling. No-one really knew how long he had been like that but more than likely, at least a couple of hours. As I had said, everyone on the yard is wary of handling Jet. Fortunately the yard manager and someone else managed to hold him, cut him out of the wire, and get him out of the rather tight space he had somehow got himself into, and led him to the yard. On the yard, having washed him down and checked him over, other than a couple of superficial cuts, incredibly, he was fine. The interesting part was; when the other yard manager explained the scenario to me on my return, she said she was genuinely amazed at how quiet he was to handle and it was as if he knew he had to trust them to help him! Whilst this is logical and many horses would react the same in such scenarios, there have been many occasions in the past with Jet when he should have known to trust people to help him out of a spot, but did not and carried on in his usual boisterous way regardless of the dangers, etc.

On my return to the yard I approached Jet with my usual caution but telling myself to have an open mind and trust him. I spoke to him the words we had agreed with Jackie, 'you trust me and I'll trust you' and started to move around him and groom him. After a while I found myself standing in his stable with his big nose in my face breathing on me but with no feeling of aggression or defensiveness from him. I actually kissed his nose for the first time ever having never dared before for fear of having my face bitten off and we stood like that for what seemed like an age.

Since then I have not felt at all frightened of Jet; we are slowly working up to picking out all four feet, but so far handling and riding him has been a pleasure.

There have been the occasional 'conversations' (explanations and confirmations) but I believe we are both making progress. I have even taken Jet out to different places in the horsebox and the trips have been totally without stress and enjoyable for both of us! Without the worry of Jet breaking loose and escaping, or me not being able to hold on to him, I hope to go to lots of different places with him for nice hacks or low-key competitions.

Going in to winter with limited turnout may become a challenge. I am hoping that Jet and I will have formed a bond that means we understand each other and will get through winter, perhaps being a little more bouncy, but we will be fine.

Jet has his new job as happy hacker; the occasional local competition; and friend, and I can't thank Jackie enough. Without Jackie's intervention, and Jet being so candid, I don't think we would have been together very much longer and Jet would have continued through life protecting himself at all costs.

It's only been three weeks and already people on the yard are surprised when they see him calmly following me around at my shoulder with or without a lead rope so hopefully his bad press will fade soon!

*****

Still watching from the realms above...

Joanne and her dog Casper

Casper was my third Bull Terrier as sadly I had lost my first two due to ill health, aged five and six-years-old. My second 'bully', Lydia, I rescued aged five and was heartbroken when I lost her due to a severe back problem when she had only been with me a year. I had found it very difficult to come to terms with her death and after six months friends persuaded me that I needed to get another dog.

After all the heartbreak, I felt I 'deserved' a puppy and contacted a Bull Terrier breeder. When I observed the litter of puppies together, Casper was by far the liveliest, the naughtiest; the clown! Since he was completely white we decided Casper would be a great name for him. For several years he proved to be a real handful, virtually impossible to train, and would have me in tears at times with his destructive behaviours! But I adored him; everyone that met him adored him. Casper had a way of 'converting' people that weren't even particularly dog lovers or lovers of his breed. He saw it as 'his job' to make friends with everyone. He was my 'big baby boy', and despite his size and heavy build, he thought nothing of jumping on my lap for a cuddle, and loved to be wrapped up in a blanket. I spoilt him rotten and he deserved it.

When my daughter Emily was born four years ago I was a bit worried that he would feel rejected but I need not have worried. Casper very gracefully accepted that 'mummy was busy' and was there by my side as always. He adored Emily and would sit by the side of her Moses basket, as if 'guarding' her. When my son Leo was born two years later, Casper knew the score and took to his 'Grandad' duties again. Casper was my 'sense of calm,' he understood my moods. If he thought I was getting too exasperated with the children, he would appear in front of me and give me a look as if to say: 'You need to calm down, Mum'! It wasn't a scolding look, more one of understanding sympathy.

By age ten, Casper started to slow down and suffered from quite bad arthritis. He was only able to walk short distances and found it difficult to walk on

Real Animal Communication Stories No.7

anything other than soft grass. A few months before he died he started to have seizures and was losing weight. I knew he was becoming poorly but I didn't want him to go through the trauma of major investigations as he found the vets so stressful. The last few days of his life he had 'lost his spark' and on the 11th December 2015 I said goodbye to my 'baby boy', and rocked him to sleep on my lap. He was thirteen years old.

I felt lost without him. Everywhere I looked he should be there but wasn't. It felt like part of me had died with him and I didn't know what to do with my grief. I was surprised also how much the children missed him. Emily would burst into tears and one day said to me, "Heaven is very naughty for taking my dog away, now we are on our own!" She asked me if we could catch the bus to Heaven and get him back. If only we could! I knew that there were psychic people that claimed to be able to contact people that had passed and started searching online for anyone that could maybe do the same for animals. To my amazement there was, and Jackie's name came up.

I must say I was sceptical but I thought I had nothing to lose and I would do anything to make contact with my boy!

On the day of my appointment I sat by the phone feeling excited but nervous; I wondered how I would deal with the disappointment if this didn't work! As soon as I heard Jackie's voice it was like I already knew her. Within seconds I knew Casper was there, it sent tingles down my spine. Jackie said she could see a picture of Casper lying on his side and he had told her 'lack of oxygen'. I immediately knew he was talking about his seizures; he would lie on his side and I would hold him until it passed. (His mouth would go a blue colour and I knew this indicated a lack of oxygen. Somehow he would get over it and go back to his normal self.) He then went on to say he was a 'big strong boy but never hurt anyone.' These had been my exact words about him in the days after his death.

He told Jackie that he didn't like walking on pebbles which was so true because of his arthritis in his later years. He had to be driven to places as he found hard surfaces sore on his toes. He was proud to say 'I am 100% trustworthy with children!' Again I was amazed because this was a phrase I had used so often when talking about him.

It took my breath away when he said he had been watching my daughter Emily writing but had noticed her gripping her pen very tightly, concentrating. Jackie asked if she was finding it hard to do, and I agreed she was. I explained that just a few days before, I had been trying to teach Emily how to hold a pen correctly; she had found it difficult and had become quite agitated. Casper, bless him, suggested she close her eyes when she is writing to see if that helps! I spoke to my daughter Emily about talking to Casper and she was thrilled to know that he had been watching her write. She tried his suggestion of writing with her eyes shut but said out loud, "Casper, I can't see what I am doing now!" This made me laugh and at least he had helped her not feel agitated anymore.

When I asked Jackie to pass on to Casper how much 'Daddy' misses him, he commented re my husband that it seemed he always leaves things to the last minute! This is so true about him that it made me laugh out loud!

Casper said that sometimes I would bump him with the cupboard doors but it was okay because I always said sorry! I knew what he was referring to straightaway because he had a habit of lying on the floor in the kitchen, and most often against the cupboard I was trying to get into!

Jackie told me that Casper was happy and then he made a joke... He said, 'I'm not a ghost, I am a spirit'! Jackie remarked how wonderfully clever that remark was, it truly tickled her. He then called himself a 'gentleman in the sky'! It warmed my heart so much to think of him being happy like this.

There was too much information given through Jackie for it to be a coincidence. I was left in no doubt that this had been my boy talking. The experience was truly amazing, life changing really. I am someone that had always hoped there was 'life after death' and that Heaven existed but I never truly believed it. I believe now, and it has given me an inner peace to know that Casper is ok, and one day we will be reunited. Emily has told me on several occasions that sometimes at night, he comes down from the sky and cuddles her. I am sure he does!

A month after the reading I was delighted to see that Jackie was working as an animal reader at a holistic fair very close to where I lived. It was so lovely to meet her in person, and I attended her inspirational talk too. It was such a joy to hear how her life was saved, and the joy that she brings to others. Although she does television and works with celebrities' pets, she was so down-to-earth and made animal communication seem so natural and uncomplicated – I could have listened to her all day! I have been inspired by what she does and would love to learn this amazing skill if I could. Not only because it would be amazing to communicate on that level with my own future pets, but also it would be so rewarding to help people connect with their spirit pets which, as I know personally, helps so much with the grieving process and gives a real sense of peace which is priceless!

*****

Such an amazing and clever little girl...

Moyra and her cat Ali

"That's it, no more cats!" I'd been a cat lover all my life (or an ailurophile, as I've recently discovered); ever since a little tabby and white cat strolled in through our front door nearly seventy years ago. I was little more than two years old and eagerly followed the little visitor down the hallway on my hands and knees, begging my less than impressed mother to allow her to stay. Tibby, as she was called (once Mum finally accepted her as part of the family), stayed with us for twelve years and became my closest friend and confidante.

When I grew up and had a home of my own many more cats followed, all loved dearly and still remembered for the joy they each brought: Gemini, Sydney, Captain, Sylvie, Neffy, and finally Dumble. I still grieve for beloved Neffy, a gentle cat who was killed by a speeding car outside our house. And for Dumble too, our adopted black cat who'd had such a hard life before ending his days with us. I nursed him through leukaemia until eventually he died after months of suffering. *No more cats. I couldn't go through all that again.*

Three years passed after Dumble left us then one day what I had dreaded, happened... my son, John-

Real Animal Communication Stories No.7

Patrick, known as Jeeps, asked if he could have another cat. He was sixteen and his girlfriend at the time wanted to get him a kitten for Christmas. I was dismayed and offered all kinds of excuses but in the end agreed, albeit reluctantly, and we arranged a visit to *Iris's Cats in Need*, our local cat sanctuary.

Iris's house was completely taken over by stray cats. We lingered there an hour or so, gazing into cages, regretfully wishing we could save them all. Not a new-born kitten in sight though – most were fully grown cats who had been lost, ill treated or abandoned. The youngest were at least six months old, a dozen or so adorable felines, all clambering noisily for attention and making it impossible for us to choose. Who should we go for – the black, the ginger or the tabby? And which black, ginger or tabby, there were so many! In the end my son made his choice, based on her being the quietest little cat in the room – ironic really because she turned out to be the most vocal animal I've ever known!

He named her Alison (Ali) and we only later discovered how appropriate that name was. She'd been found wandering the streets in a very rough neighbourhood before one of Iris's volunteers finally rescued her. Ali was indeed a real little 'alley cat.'

Once in her new home she went straight to the spot where Dumble had died. It was as though she could smell his scent or discern his presence, even after three years. Though initially very timid, especially around men, Ali has become confident and sociable and loves to make new friends. She is very affectionate and if she senses anyone is unwell or unhappy she will make a point of comforting them. Cats, like many animals, are great little healers.

We soon discovered Ali's hunting skills were virtually non-existent. In fourteen years she has never caught a bird. On the contrary, she is rather afraid of birds and will hide if one comes too close. One summer she brought home a few butterflies as trophies, carried unharmed in her soft palate. Nowadays she's a little clumsy and unable to jump too high. However, she has become a skilful footballer. Her favourite game involves ping-pong balls. She will announce her intention to play (a high pitched chirrup) and retrieve a ball (one of many) and often unreachable by human hand from under the chest or sofa. She then invites me to join in, usually while I'm busy in the kitchen. She waits, poised like a playful puppy – the rule being that after a count of three I throw and she catches (which she always does perfectly) and then dribbles with the ball until it becomes hidden once more from sight. I then have to scrabble around on my hands and knees to find another and thus begins the 'one, two, three' game again. Maybe I should teach her a few more numbers now she's mastered three. It's great exercise for Ali but not so great for my knees!

She talks vociferously, rather like an Oriental cat; not so much meowing as chatting, and mostly with Jeeps whom she adores. She will hold forth at some length when we return home, telling us about her day perhaps or her plans for the evening! She has recently taken to looking wise and inscrutable, posing in the attitude of a sphinx. Maybe she fancies herself as an Egyptian temple cat. She must surely have a fascinating ancestry.

Last year, Ali, then fourteen but still looking and behaving like a kitten, was diagnosed with hyperthyroidism and has to have tablets to lower her thyroxin levels. More recently she began to have seizures in her sleep which alarmed us and initially caused her a lot of anxiety and distress. Because of her age our vet thought the cause would most likely be a brain tumour and prescribed steroids and anti-seizure medication. For some reason though my son and I both doubted this diagnosis and felt uneasy about administering the drugs. I didn't know, of course, but wondered if the seizures might be vascular in origin. We decided to adopt a 'wait and see' attitude. I was unwell at the time and had become very worried about Ali's condition, fearing we might lose her imminently. I kept imagining life without little Ali, something that I know has to be faced at some point. The grief was unbearable.

It was at this point I decided to seek a second opinion. I'd been interested in animal communication for some time so I was convinced that I would find someone special who could communicate with Ali; someone who could interpret her own needs and preferences and thus help us to decide what action to take. I searched online to find a local communicator but every time was drawn back to one name: Jackie Weaver, the well-known TV animal psychic.

To my surprise I found that Jackie offers very reasonable telephone and Skype consultations. It couldn't have been easier. I sent off an email, expecting to receive an automated reply in a week's time if I was lucky. To my delight, Jackie herself responded – within five minutes or so!

I was offered an appointment for the following week and meanwhile had to send a photo of Ali, together with a few basic details. Suddenly I felt easier, intuitively aware that a lot of help was already on its way.

When Jackie phoned it was like hearing from an old friend. I felt completely at ease. Jackie explained that the communication was all through pictures, aided, of course, by her own beloved cat in Spirit, Stan. She wasted no time in getting to the cause of Ali's problem. Ali was showing her the right side of her neck – there seemed to be an occasional problem with blood flow (exactly as I'd felt intuitively). Ali was quite adamant that we should not be too concerned about this and said, "Tell my mum not to worry!" and explained that she was not bothered by these episodes. She also revealed that she didn't want to take the steroids. Aware that she was already drinking a lot because of the overactive thyroid, she felt that they would cause her to drink more.

She went on to give further reassurance that suggested a tumour was unlikely. She clarified this by stating, "I think my weight is stable. When I lost it, that was my thyroid; my eyes are even (meaning the pupils are equal) I'm not favouring my head – my head isn't tilting." And best of all, "I don't act senile, do I?" These were all exactly as she said, and made perfect sense to me.

Apparently Ali was very worried about possible side effects from medications and in her opinion,"What happens to me, happens and at present I have no side effects." Her attitude to the anti-seizure medication was, "I don't want to take anything that will slur my words!" By this time we were both laughing and the fun continued as she described more about herself to Jackie by saying, "I'm very sweet and just like a kitten – stroke me, please. I'm very nosy. What are you doing?" Then, "I stay close to home; I don't go anywhere." This was interesting. Last year when she began to have seizures we decided to have new fencing installed in the garden. We covered it with mesh to keep her safe in her own little space.

She showed herself making 'kitteny, loving eyes' at Jeeps (she is such a little flirt and adores him, even when he plays rough and chases her, which she enjoys!). "I'm such a little person!" (The best possible description of her!). And, "I'm so loved – but I give love too!" She described Jeeps as having a deep voice and being very good with numbers. We figured out that this would be a result of his daily weight training – counting repetitions of lifts.

Ali is also aware that I 'call in energies' as she put it. This refers to the fact that I'm a Spiritual healer and offer up prayers for her every night before going upstairs to bed.

Surprisingly she added, "Blackie comes to visit. Ask Blackie to help..." This was so amazing as dear Dumble had actually been called Blackie by a previous owner. This offering by Ali was so poignant as some years ago when I was ill, I had a visitation one night. He told me, "You helped me when I was ill, now I have come to help you." Friends have often commented that they had just caught sight of a black cat, passing through. Our Dumble still likes to visit us, it seems. Bless you Dumble.

Finally, Ali summed up her own conversation with, "Follow your intuition. I still got good energy in me. I'm coping fine. I'm still your little girl." I tell her this every day and Jackie reminded me to continue to do so whenever she rubs her face close onto us. It will mean the world to her!

Since the session with Jackie, Ali has seemed happier and more settled than ever. We all are, in fact. She still has occasional episodes, or 'triggers' as she describes them, but is no longer troubled by them. They tend to come in clusters but she recovers quickly.

Meeting Jackie Weaver has been a terrific investment; I have always believed that our relationship with animals is a vital factor in our, and their, evolution on this planet. Having experienced an animal communication with Jackie, I see that she provides a priceless service to animals and their human companions in this cycle of life.

For us, it has been possible to think ahead to a time when Ali is no longer with us physically, while still fully enjoying her presence with us now. We have even found the perfect resting place for her in our garden; somewhere we can always remember our delightful and precious friend.

*****

When pets spot the chance to talk...

Rebecca and her cat Nefertiti and Co!

In early 2005 when we first moved into the house where we currently live here in the USA, my family had only one pet: my mother's Scarlet Macaw named Blaze. After having had at least one dog in the family for the past 20 years we had not had one since losing Frisker a few years prior to 2005. Without at least one dog, we all felt something was missing in our lives but we didn't want to bring another one into the family until we had settled into our new house. Also, having lost contact with the breeder from whom we had got our first three dogs, we were 'out of the loop' as far as finding a new breeder that wasn't several states away. After we moved we felt that we couldn't afford to have the back yard fenced in. We had always had dogs of a breed that enjoyed running and playing in the back yard, so without a fence, it would not have been safe to let a dog do those things. Blaze was (and is) a beautiful girl, but birds are not at all cuddly pets! We missed having a furry family member to pet and snuggle, but soldiered on as best we could.

Sometimes in life our needs are met in mysterious ways we didn't even know were possible. During the first spring and summer in our new house we often saw a tabby cat in the woods in our back yard, but she was very skittish. Just her ears and eyes were most often what we saw of her! One day in the fall (autumn) as I was leaving for work, I saw her beneath the bird feeders. Hoping to distract her from eating any of our backyard feathered friends, I put out a plate of cat food for her and left for work. That evening she came to the door to the deck to see if the 'restaurant' was open for dinner! I brought out another plate of food for her and that was that: she became our kitty.

We thought we'd never be able to have a cat because of my dad's allergies, but gradually she was allowed access to more rooms in the house with no adverse affects to my dad's health. (His allergist later told us that sometimes people can grow out of or become more or less immune to certain allergens.) The name we chose for her was Nefertiti because she was slim and had a regal appearance like the cats in ancient Egyptian hieroglyphics. The next spring a second kitty, a black one we named Carbon, joined our family.

In 2008 we were finally able to add a dog to the family again and adopted our current dog, Zoe. (The chance to adopt her came along a bit sooner than we had planned, so we had to rush to put up a fence around the back yard so she could go out and play without having to be on a leash!) The person who relinquished Zoe, a fluffy grey, black and white dog breed called a Keeshond to rescue, claimed that she was spayed but a few months after we adopted her she went into heat so we knew that hadn't been the truth! When we had her spayed our vet told us that it was apparent Zoe had been bred from more than once.

She had also been abused and was initially terrified of anyone, especially a man, carrying even a single sheet of paper. It took her years to relax into our family and not be so anxious all the time. She adored my mom and followed her everywhere like a shadow, thus earning the nickname "The Velcro Dog!" Zoe and Nefertiti ended up being best friends and could often be found hanging around together and even playing a 'chase me' sort of game. Nefertiti would run right in front of Zoe in a teasing manner and Zoe was supposed to chase after her. Once Nefertiti was outside and being scolded by the flock of crows that lives in the woods behind our house. She stomped into the house in disgust and went to find Zoe, who went trotting right out into the back yard to bark at the crows! Nefertiti called in reinforcements!

In May of 2014 we found out that Nefertiti had cancer. We took her to a veterinary oncologist and did oral chemotherapy to try to keep her happy and comfortable. Remembering what Jackie had said in the past about animals being able to understand so much when we talk to them, so we told the rest of the pets, "All of us are made up of cells, and some of Nefertiti's are sick so we are giving her medicine to help her feel better. None of you can catch the

Real Animal Communication Stories No.7

sickness she has." Although we did everything we could do for her and she had quite possibly the best summer ever, we lost her that October. Even when you know something like that is coming; it's still terribly difficult when it happens. All of my family had a rough time dealing with the loss of Nefertiti, so about a month after she passed, Mom and I made arrangements to have Jackie help us chat with Carbon, Zoe and Blaze to find out how they were coping too.

We began by chatting with Carbon, who said, "I'm fine and getting on with life as we do." She referred to Nefertiti as "Neffie" when she talked about her and mentioned at one point during our conversation that Neffie was sitting on the end of the bed. Carbon told Jackie that, "It was a prolonged process, but we understood." She gave Jackie the impression that there were a lot of ups and downs, which there were, especially at the end. According to Carbon they all sort of 'watched from afar' and gave us space to deal with it and give Neffie the extra care and attention she needed. In Neffie's absence, Carbon told Jackie that she wasn't lonely, but was still adjusting. We asked if she was okay being the only kitty or if she would like a playmate. Carbon said, "Not now," giving Jackie the impression that she can amuse herself. Also, she said that Mom wouldn't cope with a new pet. Just five weeks after her passing was, "Too soon, too soon," she told us. I asked how we would know if she changed her mind and would like a playmate? Carbon showed Jackie the image of a cat walking on a path to our house which we took as a way of indicating that another pet would be guided to us at the time we were meant to get one, so we should let the future unfold.

Next we chatted to our dog Zoe. "I understood what was going on with Neffie and I was even more loving," she said. Mom and I agreed that she definitely comforted us during Neffie's illness. At the very beginning of Neffie's illness, Zoe pointed out that Mom had an intuitive feeling that something was wrong, and also said she understood it was a very hard time. She shared, "There were lots of questions upon questions upon questions." Since Neffie's passing Zoe told us that she has tried to fill the gap left by Neffie, and Mom (also involved in the call) related how Zoe and Neffie were best friends. When asked how she is doing now that Neffie is gone physically, Zoe showed Jackie the door from the house to the deck and said Neffie can go through the door now without needing to have it opened! It was around that point in the conversation that Jackie remarked that she got all goose-pimply because she could feel that Neffie was really listening in to the conversation as well. The next thing we knew, she had taken over Jackie's chat with Zoe!

Neffie told us she has a "smooth coat now," indicating that her fur was back to normal in Heaven. (At one of the initial appointments with the veterinary oncologist we had an ultrasound done to check for additional tumours and it was necessary to shave her tummy for that procedure. The fur never did grow all back.) Jackie was told that Neffie visited Mom in a dream and Mom confirms that it did indeed happen. "Was me, was me!" Neffie says. She wanted us to know, "You couldn't have done more for me - you had such hope and loads of prayers." I pointed out that we did ask people to pray for her. Then Neffie showed Jackie how Mom wrote a prayer for us to say after we buried her, and said how Mom saved it in a box. "It was time for me to move on," she tells us. "I really did pick up with the treatment and then it went down again." We agreed that her last summer with us was her best summer ever. She was also very tolerant of the treatments; to the point that all the vets that helped us treat her during those few months remarked how sweet she was.

She then talks about how she was very regal like an Egyptian queen and she liked to be petted very slowly. She says how she played with Zoe but would say "Uh, me first please!" when it came to receiving attention and so on. Jackie remarked that it really wasn't a surprise for Neffie to take over Zoe's reading. Zoe butted back in with, "Okay, I'll just take the back seat!" About Zoe, Neffie said she was doing good and proud to have taught her how to have confidence. When it was time for her to draw back, Neffie said to Jackie, "I'm going back, I've got to go, I'm schmoozing with the locals." Mom laughed and said we'd be happy when she could come back again for another visit. "I come back and forth," she said. After that, the chat returned to Zoe.

Zoe showed Jackie how she greets us when we come home, then remarked that Mom hadn't been sleeping well and told her it would get better and settle back down. Then she said that Mom had "needless worries" about a lot of 'what-ifs' with Neffie and that she and the rest of us need to let go of such feelings. Zoe cleverly pointed out that she used to be a worrier and we helped her come out of it, so now the tables have turned and she says we, particularly Mom – must try not to worry. Zoe's last comments before the end of her 'turn' were that we (but especially Mom) had been very brave through a sad situation and she was proud of us. Mom asked Jackie to thank her and tell her that we love her very much and she's very important to us. "I know I'm loved," said Zoe, "I'm told every day."

As previously mentioned, we wondered if another cat would come into our lives and this seemed to be symbolised by the 'vision' of a cat walking up our path. Well... Almost a year later the path turned out to be the driveway of a friend's house. I had stopped by to drop off her keys after taking care of her house and dogs while she and her husband were out of town. When I got out of my car in her driveway, two friendly little characters came running up to me! My friend and I checked with her neighbour but the kittens didn't belong to them. They seemed to have appeared out of nowhere; no one had seen them before. While we tried to find out if they belonged to anyone, we put down a bowl of water for them and they were so thirsty they drank for a solid minute at least. Not wanting them to be hit by a car or eaten by predators, I called Mom who came over with a carrier to bring them to our house where they would be safe, and at our house is where they stayed! Mom says she knew they were meant for us from the moment I said, "One is black like Carbon, and one is striped like Neffie was!" We truly believe they were sent to us and that it was meant to be.

*****

A true and adorable Prince...

Donna and her horse Blue

In 2001, I went to view a horse called Blue. He was a Connemara and said to be an eight-year-old. When I saw his beautiful sleek face over the stable door I just knew he was the one. Sadly I couldn't take him there

Real Animal Communication Stories No.7

and then as he had been kicked by another horse and was lame.

Two weeks went past, which seemed to be forever, then I got the call to go and try him. Yes, he was fresh as a daisy, but he just felt so right. The following day I went to collect him. I was so excited to get him home.

We moved around quite a bit but the place where we eventually settled was lovely and by this time we had developed a relationship that was just inseparable; he was the most amazing genuine loving horse. I could leave him days un-ridden and then just tack him up and go out and he would never put a foot wrong. All of my friends loved him and he was a stunner too!

He was loved by all the children and I trusted him with any child on board as I knew implicitly that he would look after them, and he always did.

Blue seemed to be a silent horse, as I never heard him whinny, not until Willow, my old mare, and his companion, had to be put to sleep. That was the first time I heard him when sadly he was calling for her. That made my heart melt as he did have a little voice after all, and I comforted him for the loss of his friend, and my own dear girl.

Blue was one of a kind; he was just perfect in every way and I loved him and I think he loved me too. Our sixteen years we spent together had been just perfect.

Blue never really needed a vet over the years I had him, until the last week of his life. One day, I just knew something wasn't right. It was a cold day yet I noticed him lying down in the mud, which wasn't like him at all. I called the vets and they promptly came out. They examined him and said he had colic caused by impaction, which they treated him for over the next few days. On 12th February 2016 (my wedding anniversary) they gave him the all clear. I was so relieved for the two reasons: firstly, my boy was better, and secondly, my husband and I were due to go away to Belgium to celebrate our anniversary.

The next day, Saturday, I stayed with him all morning. I spent quality time with him and also sorted out everything for him: his stable, his feeds, and left notes about pain relief for my friend and my daughter who were caring for him while I was away, in case he needed any. I went down the field to Blue and he was fine, swishing his tail and grazing happily. I felt comfortable to leave him as he seemed to well again. I gave him a big hug and said I would be back on Monday.

We went on our anniversary trip and that evening when I managed to get onto Wi-Fi, I checked in to see how he was. I was told he was okay but deep down, I just wanted to be home. The Sunday, Valentine's Day, I checked in on him again and my daughter said he had been reluctant to go into his stable and didn't eat his tea from the previous night. I said not to worry as long as he had hay and was grazing.

I was on my journey back over the Sunday night and arrived back the Monday morning. I couldn't wait to get home as had been struggling to get a signal on my phone that morning and then lots of messages came through. I glanced at my phone and just saw, 'so sorry to hear'. I just went into complete melt down. My husband took my phone off me and said to wait to look at it until we got out of passport control. I

Real Animal Communication Stories No.7

shrieked and asked him to give me my phone, but he declined. I said, "It's Blue isn't it?" I instantly knew it was, and that he had gone. I couldn't control myself – I just wanted to get to him.

When I got home, I changed my shoes and raced up to the field. I struggled for breath as I walked to his stable door. I looked in; he was lying there, lifeless. My world had just been torn apart. I lay with him asking, "Why?" I just couldn't understand it as it looked as though he had just gone in, lain down, gone to sleep and then never woken up. All sorts of questions crossed my mind: Why, when, how? Things I just couldn't answer. I was lost.

Arrangements were made for him to be removed for which I couldn't stay. I was so desperate to have him cremated but my funds wouldn't allow this.

As days went past, I just couldn't understand why this had happened. It was so frustrating for me as my soul mate had gone and I had no answers. All I knew was that my heart had been broken into a million pieces. I do have other horses but the loss was greater with Blue than I had ever felt before. I searched the internet looking for answers and came across Jackie. I whirred it round and round in my brain but eventually plucked up the courage to book her as I do believe in the afterlife but I still found it very hard.

Jackie got back in touch to book the following week. That week went so slowly as I knew I would have answers. When the day finally came, I felt sick, I was shaking but also relieved. The phone rang and it was Jackie, my heart was racing.

Jackie communicated with Blue and the conversation was just awesome.

Jackie got the feeling from Blue that he was a gentle soul and genuine. Yes indeed, that was spot on. He mentioned the name 'Prince'. I couldn't validate the name until Jackie said she thought it was about a book and I will come across it. And I would! Oh my God, I remembered as a child I bought a book and it was called *Prince Amongst Ponies.* Jackie asked if I had this to hand. I did and I went and got it. My dream horse was on the cover of the book and it was Blue's double in his younger days! Oh my goodness – I could not believe it!

Blue then went on about a ball that seemed to be sitting in something. I used to put a ball in the waters in winter to help with easier drinking when frozen! Blue was making us smile as he mentioned a mouse in his stable. I asked why he mentioned it and he replied he found it amusing to watch.

Jackie asked if I wanted to ask anything and said I really wanted to know why and how? She said she would ask and relayed to me that Blue told her he just went in and lay down, went to sleep and then he crossed over. He also said it was nothing to do with anything else at all and Jackie said she thought the stable was untouched. I totally agreed as I can say it wasn't disturbed at all. So bless him, he had done what I thought, well hoped, and by what I had seen, he had simply lain down and gone to sleep forever.

I asked how old Blue actually was as my records showed he was twenty but he quickly said twenty-four, which Jackie was quick to say could be wrong

Real Animal Communication Stories No.7

as they often don't see age like we do. But actually, having looked into it, I can validate that now.

Blue was showing a gilet a plain looking one and yes, I did have one and I used to ride him with it on.

Jackie said she thought I had had him cremated. I said I wanted to but couldn't afford it. Jackie was a little confused as she told me she was sure Blue had said, 'He was scattered now'. I actually understood this as he would have been cremated with all the other animals that day which I explained to Jackie.

I said, "I'm surprised Madam (another horse) hasn't come through." Jackie said that Blue had just told her that she was a very sick horse. Bless her, she most certainly was. Blue mentioned that I would have been hysterical if I had had to make 'that decision' so many people have to make for their horse. He was so right and, as sad as I am that he has gone, but what a blessing he went so peacefully and as nature intended.

Blue told Jackie that he loved me very much, and my sweet voice, and if he came back to visit that he would be behind me. She mentioned I often look at a tree that seems to have a robin that visits. Yes indeed I do and a little robin visits very often. Jackie said that it is sent as a reminder from Blue as the tree is in front of his stable.

My reading with Jackie and Blue was just so calming; it most certainly has helped me with the grieving process. It has given me peace of mind, knowing that he is okay and the answers I got have given me the assurances I needed.

It has given me a new light to know that they do go on in a spirit life – and although they are not here with us physically they are still around us, just in a different way.

I would definitely call Jackie again, knowing that she can communicate with animals so accurately. Then all my fur babies could speak to me and let me know they are happy and okay. I cannot thank her enough for the conversation with my beloved Blue.

*****

Everybody's friend...

Mel and her dog Ozzie

I first met Ozzie at a rescue centre. I had a phone call to say there was a nine-month-old Lurcher who had been there a while and was not settling. I had really wanted a Whippet, but I said I would go and meet him anyway.

Well, the moment I saw him, I finally knew what love at first sight meant! He was pure white, barely more than skin and bone, and had the most gorgeous hazel eyes that implored me to get him out of there. Needless to say, I did and our lovely journey began.

The first hurdle to get over was, would he get on with my Siamese cat Reuben? As I led Ozzie into the house, the cat yelled at him and poor Ozzie looked dumbstruck! I didn't know if he had come across cats before but the boundaries had been set – this cat was in charge! And that is the way it stayed.

It wasn't all plain sailing though, Oz certainly had a mind of his own. We went to training classes and he would behave impeccably do everything that was asked of him, walking to heal, recall all perfect.

Real Animal Communication Stories No.7

Then, back on the street, he would pull on the lead, turn a deaf ear when out in the fields and with his long Lurcher legs he just wanted to have his freedom. He loved to run, and run he did! He ran so far that he ended up on the road until someone was quick enough to catch him with me puffing and panting up the rear. Some more training was required and due to his playful spirit, complete with the odd dash for freedom, we made lots friends along the way.

Eventually, Ozzie became well known as he would exercise the other dogs in the neighbourhood! He would run and they would chase him and he loved it because he knew they could never catch up with him! Everyone we met would have to stroke him and tell him what a handsome boy he was and he would smile his doggie smile and my heart would swell with love and pride.

Ozzie's favourite place was called Bewl Water, which is a large reservoir. We would sometimes go there with friends and they would swim and Oz would paddle. He liked the water but he didn't want to go too deep but he made up for it by splashing about and woofing at the other dogs as they made their way in and out the water.

Oz had another attribute – he was very gentle and empathetic. He loved the donkeys we would pass on our morning walk and they would come to the gate and rub noses with him and he hated to see anyone in distress. We where out in the fields one day when he kept barking from a distance and I found him standing next to a large Deer that had passed away. Ozzie was crying and I told him it was too late to help but he wouldn't budge and I eventually had to drag him away. He kept looking back and cried most of the way home.

He was also a homeboy who loved his home comforts: His bed (mine) and the sofa (ours) and he would lay with me all evening snuggled up under his very own little duvet. When it was treat time he would shake his head 'No' until the preferred treat was offered!

Eleven years passed with lots of love and laughter then one day, I saw a lump on his right fore leg. I immediately got a vet to look at it, and sadly, a biopsy confirmed it was Cancer. We went to a specialist who said the best thing was for Ozzie to have his leg amputated to give him the best chance of a more prolonged life. After some more tests, the operation went ahead and Oz came back home on what was Good Friday that year. He adapted well to having three legs and was soon running faster than his doggie friends. He was so happy and gained even more admiring attention from people we met.

Sadly, within a couple of months of his amputation, I was extremely concerned to find some lumps on his side that had suddenly appeared. Devastatingly, these were proved to be malignant. Oz slowed down, and was in pain, and I could see the sorrow in his eyes that had replaced that sparkle that always shone from him. My heart was breaking, I couldn't believe this was happening but I knew that I had to make the call that would take my best friend and soul mate away, from me. Oz was put to sleep with me by his side and the love of my life had gone.

I was devastated and inconsolable. I needed help to get through the grief and I found Jackie's book *Animal Communication from Heaven and Earth* helped so much but I needed more proof from my boy. I got in touch with Jackie and we arranged a time when we could have a 'chat' with my Oz.

Jackie rang and Oz came through quickly and passed on his message that he was 'alive and well and like a statue'. He always sat with a very elegant pose so I understood what he meant. Jackie asked me if he had had an accident to his right front paw as he seemed to be indicating like he had broken a toe, or something similar. I told her that he had a toe missing on that foot due to an injury. What confirmation!

He said he was the gentlest dog ever, so knowing like an old soul would be, and never hurt anyone. He declared, "I was a people pleaser and greeted everyone." Jackie asked him why he went to Heaven and he told her it was an illness and he had 'cell breakdown'. She gently asked me if I understood it, to which I replied I did. He went on further to say, "It was spreading around my body but I coped really well. There was nothing my Mum could do to help me and I was put to sleep peacefully." I thanked him for that. He said that I was burdened with guilt and that I shouldn't be and Jackie said that he really wants me to let that go, I said that I now would.

Oz told Jackie he was very grateful to me and was allowed to do what he wanted and showed her himself laying stretched out on the sofa. He said he was a gentleman and always waited for me to give him what was left over on my plate. He did and who could have ever refused those gorgeous hazel eyes.

He showed Jackie the reservoir at Bewl, which he loved. Jackie started to giggle and then hesitated but said that she would just tell me what she thought he was trying to put across. He was mentioning that my car was rather old and was making noises? I laughed and agreed. Oz said that I was fine about it as long as it gets me from 'A to B'. That made me laugh more because I said those were often the very words I said to Oz when we went in the car hoping it would keep going, and it always did!

Oz said that I kissed his head saying, "You're my boy." I responded and he said, "I am your boy." He told Jackie that even though he is in spirit he still comes and sits in my bedroom. At that point, my cat Reuben started to meow and Oz said, "That cat has been short changed!" When Jackie asked him what he meant, he said it referred to Reuben's 'brain department!' That was another laughter moment, and very apt. Oz mentioned Megan, a young girl he knew who came to visit him after his operation, and said she was upset. It was lovely to hear from him how special she is and how he appreciated her thoughtfulness.

He told Jackie that I was volunteering and he was proud of me! I had just started to walk the dogs at the rescue centre. How amazing is that? I am so delighted that he can see what I am doing and it gives me great satisfaction to help in a place that gave me him and made my life so very wonderful and complete. He said our energy and souls are locked together, he knew I loved 'the bones of him'. He told Jackie that when the time is right I will get another dog and he will guide me when the time is right. He said how lucky he felt having come to me.

After our chat with Jackie, I felt a weight had been lifted from me. I had proof that my wonderful boy is well and okay and that he is healed. There is no doubt in my mind that Jackie was able to communicate with Ozzie because he told her so much detail about himself and our time together. She even gave me things that over time I had myself forgotten and it is lovely to know that he is watching over me and still with me.

Jackie has a special gift she is a truly remarkable lady. I came off the phone knowing what a kind down-to-earth lady Jackie is whose other gift is to help those who suffer so much guilt over the loss of our beloved pets. Thank you from the bottom of my heart.

*****

Definitely not 'bird-brained'...

Suzanne and her hawk Nariel

Nariel, my Harris' Hawk, came into my life at 16 weeks old. I opened her carry box to find her on her back, feet in the air, with her weapons of mass destruction (claws, very big claws) pointing in my direction! How we moved on from this to the beautiful calm hawk that I can actually have on my bare arm is a long story! I have to say; it was probably more to do with her good nature rather than my ability as a falconer at that time. She was my first hawk – and the love of my life. To have a hawk trust you, is one of the greatest privileges that can be bestowed on you.

Nariel and I have hunted together for over nine years. I have been questioned from time to time – how an animal lover can hunt with a hawk. My simple and humble answer is that God, or nature, made her a hunter and eater of meat. She cannot eat anything else or be anything else – who am I to question God or Mother Nature? We hunt until she has what she wants to eat and nothing more. My reward is that I get to link minds with her, take to the woods and be a hawk for a few hours, forgetting my human concerns.

All was well, until Nariel developed an obsession for biting at her wing, even so far as to damage the muscle and leave an awful gaping sore. Many trips to the vets ensued – no parasites found, drugs tried, beak adaptations done – nothing seemed to work. She was not doing it from boredom as she regularly flew and she was free in a huge aviary with lovely views over the valley. I tried putting her in with a male and she had some babies but sadly, they died. However, despite all efforts, it got to the stage where I could not allow her to carry on self-mutilating and I had to contemplate the unthinkable.

I had been reading one of Jackie Weaver's books, as I had just lost my beloved ginger tom, Ptolemy. The book mentioned that Jackie could communicate with living creatures also. I'm open to lots of things that others may consider 'weird', but I don't accept anything without proof. I decided I had to try it with Nariel and see what would come up in a communication with her.

Jackie rang me at the allotted time, she was friendly and comforting – she connected with Nariel and the first words she said was that Nariel was telling her, 'I'm not neurotic!' Jackie was nonplussed by this comment, but I knew exactly what she meant. The reason was that the vet was treating Nariel with anti-psychotic drugs which had been successful with other birds that have an obsessive tendency to self-mutilate. I had doubted his train of thought and had a hard time believing that Nariel was doing it because she was unhappy or stressed, etc. This was not because it made me feel a failure, but because my Nariel had always been the calmest, most unstressed hawk I'd ever known!

As Jackie's conversation with Nariel went on, Jackie asked me if Nariel had a problem with her right wing. That is exactly where the wound was! Nariel showed Jackie things crawling on her feathers and I suspected this could be true. I had long wondered if Nariel could have had a parasite problem, because it coincided with her sitting on eggs. Understandably, this went un-noticed, as by the time she came off the eggs, the pecking at the wound had gone too far and become a habit (or vicious circle) of biting, hurting and biting that she couldn't stop.

Nariel told Jackie that she did not kill her previous babies and that they were 'cold' and 'just died and she didn't know why'. I did wonder if this was because the male hawk was not good at passing food and she had to keep leaving them to feed herself. This was comforting to know, as I wasn't sure what had happened to them. Nariel also told Jackie that her last lot of eggs hadn't developed and I agreed that that would make sense, as she seemed to be sat there for so long, but with no joy. Jackie said she heard, '42' and asked if that is how long hawks sit for. I said the norm is around 32 days but I was sure I had noted it in my diary and thought it was 42 days. I checked my diary and it was exactly 42 days!

Something that made me giggle – Jackie said Nariel showed her lots of water gushing into her aviary and Jackie wondered if there had been a flood? I couldn't think of anything like that and said I couldn't understand that one but, when I got off the phone, I remembered that just before Jackie called I had hosed Nariel's aviary down with water. So, of course to Nariel up on her perch, it would look like lots of water gushing below her like a flood and now I see why she doesn't like me doing it much!

Nariel said to Jackie, "I blink a lot," which Jackie did giggle about when telling me, as it sounded a rather strange thing to say but, this is true! If a hawk holds your gaze, that would be aggressive, so blinking is passive. The falconer and the hawk will glance at each other or, as Nariel and I have developed, an exaggerated blink to show respect. Such a small thing but more proof to me that actually psychic communication is possible.

Jackie then said that Nariel seems to be looking intently at the ground which was probably her aviary? Oh she does! This is because she has a mole in her aviary and it fascinates her when the earth starts moving but lucky for the mole, she doesn't fancy eating it.

What really confirmed to me that Jackie was in touch with Nariel is that the things she relayed were very much matter of fact. Had Jackie waxed lyrical and told me how much Nariel loved me etc. etc. I would have known that wasn't true; Hawks don't 'love' the falconer – they trust, like and enjoy our company, but it could never be called love.

As a result of the call with Jackie, I have been trying soothing homeopathic treatments (something that Jackie mentioned thought might help) for the wound, using a painkiller from the vet and my beautiful calm hawk is very much improving. If this continues, and I have no reason to believe that it won't, the plan is for her to have a new partner for 2017, as she told Jackie that she wanted to have more babies and another of her kind to keep her company. I will keep my promise of arranging for her food to be near her nest, as she told Jackie she did not want to leave her babies to get her food if her partner doesn't bring it to her.

Incidentally, NARIEL is the Hebrew word for the Angel who is the ruler of the noon day wind.

We are on track now for flying again in October 2016, when Nariel will be the Ruler of the Noon Day

Real Animal Communication Stories No.7

Wind once again. Thank you Jackie and I will be in touch again.

*****

Small girl with a huge personality...

Sema and her dog Smiley

Since such an early age I remember always wanting a dog and would constantly pester my parents and siblings. To me, a dog would make my life complete. Along with my love and passion for animals and wanting to help them, I achieved my goal of becoming a veterinary nurse. Thanks to this I could now prove to my parents I was old enough and wise enough to get my dog, just as I always wanted.

Being a veterinary nurse I came across so many animals needing homes. It was not until I was 23 years old, and whilst working for a charity, I came across the gentlest, yet cheeky, happiest little Yorkshire Terrier called Smiley. We found each other during the summer months of 2007 – it was a time in my life when huge changes were taking place.

Of all the dogs I came across while working, I never expected to get a Yorkie. She was brought to the charity centre for rehoming. It was through no fault of her own but as a result of her previous owner passing away. After several weeks of fostering, and the near possibility of her being rehomed to someone else, she finally came to live with me, and of course my family too. Smiley was six-years-old and she proved that being little was not going to stop her having such a big personality and a heart filled with love.

From the moment I brought her home her personality shone, and most of all her smile was priceless. As her name so fittingly describes, Smiley would actually, to my surprise, really smile! The next eight years I was to spend with her proved to be the most joyful and fulfilling of times.

She was generally a healthy little soul and naturally as the years went by, she began to slow down. It was only when she reached the age of twelve did she have a major setback. It was one evening while I was studying at home and she was in the room with me. Suddenly she rolled onto her side and began to move and shake uncontrollably. Thanks to my veterinary knowledge, I knew she was having a seizure. When she came out of it, she was debilitated, with a head tilt and completely paralysed. I was so upset. However, she was a strong and courageous little terrier and amazingly made a wonderful recovery! It was not that long before she was back to her normal, cheeky, bold self. After her recovery I was so overwhelmed that she had made it through what seemed the impossible, so taking her for her walks seemed ever more so special, knowing that she could have stayed completely paralysed. Unbelievably, shortly after this she was diagnosed with kidney failure and hypothyroidism and also needed medication for her heart. Despite her ill health, she still tried to chase the squirrels in the park and enjoyed being made a fuss of by passers by. Yet, at the same time, she was slowing down and her years were beginning to show.

One year following she had another major seizure. I rushed her to my veterinary work place and they gave her the necessary emergency treatment. This time she was struggling more than she should have been and the emergency drugs did not seem to be taking much effect. It appeared that her central nervous system was beginning to shut down and to my complete despair she was showing no signs of improvement. I stroked her and began talking to her, and sending her thoughts of great comfort in the hope she knew I was there with her. Her breathing then stopped for a moment and she began vomiting; she was now critical and was struggling to breathe. My vet looked at me and prompted me to make the hardest decision I would ever have to make. I made the most heartbreaking decision to end her suffering. I held her in my arms while she was let go, my heart felt immensely heavy and sank so deeply. Words were not able to describe the pain I felt: complete loss and feeling of emptiness.

Losing my Smiley was a hard struggle and my strength to go to work had disappeared. I thought about her every day. Somehow I couldn't quite understand how a bond so strong could just end in a matter of moments once she had passed away. I began researching mediums that were able to speak to animals that had left this Earth and luckily I found Jackie. I wasn't too sure what to expect, as I had never done this for any of my animals, but I had a strong feeling that the connection between Smiley and me had not ended. Once Jackie and I spoke and arranged a date, I felt a little more at ease.

The day she carried out the spirit reading via Skype was so overwhelming. Everything we discussed and the things she told me were so correct; unless you lived with my dog there were things Jackie mentioned that no-one else would have known. The first thing that Jackie said was that Smiley said, "Hi Mummy!" This was touching and I knew exactly why. Jackie described how Smiley was showing her a small round bed, a window to the left that she looks out of, and also described that a blanket would be put over her. These first three descriptions that Smiley showed Jackie were so very poignant, as Smiley's bed was placed in my room and it was round. The window that she looked out of was again in my room; she would sit on the window ledge or just in front of it, and watch everything that went by – it was like her television screen. Lastly, the blanket being put over was so right as I would actually tuck her in bed! Smiley was giving Jackie accurate descriptions of what she and I would do, especially within my room. She also mentioned to Jackie that I liked drawing and was artistic. This did take me by surprise, as this is something I very rarely mentioned to people, and when I did draw, Smiley would lie beside me quietly and calmly. In addition to this she was showing Jackie a certificate I had which related to my studying. Smiley was describing my certificate in veterinary nursing of exotics. I would also always speak to Smiley and tell her what we were doing or going to do and Smiley told me this really helped her.

She also showed Jackie all her teeth and was grinning. This made me laugh as her name, so fittingly, was Smiley, and when she passed away she still had all her teeth! She would do this to let me know she was still a very happy dog. In addition to this she said she was 'precious' and was 'Mummy's little baby'. This delighted me as I would always jokingly tell my parents how she was my child and I would actually tell them she was 'Mummy's little baby'. They would laugh, but I am sure they thought I was a little barmy.

Smiley told me she would 'never be alone' and would always be 'loved by two people'. This was so

Real Animal Communication Stories No.7

very important for me to know because, as strange as it sounds, I worried and thought about how she would be on her own when she passed away. However, as mentioned earlier on, her previous owner had passed away, hence the re-homing. Smiley assured me that she was not alone as she was now in contact again with her previous owner, which made me feel so much more at ease.

Jackie spoke of a 'heart shaped pillow' and said Smiley was showing her this. I had to pause to think about this and then realised the heart shaped object was the shape of the urn I now had for Smiley. She informed us that that was the 'right one to choose' and that 'her ashes were handled with great care'. This was ever more so meaningful to me, as when I chose the urn it was the one that stood out for me – it reminded me of Smiley as she had a slightly enlarged heart, and a huge loving heart too.

She mentioned that we were 'meant to be together' and that we were 'connected souls'. When Jackie said this to me I felt so very touched and knew this was true, as I had a dream about Smiley before I got her. Therefore I knew we were meant to be for each other.

Smiley also explained to me she was 'proud of me' and said, "I'm still here." I believe she certainly is still around us as she also mentioned to Jackie that I would be going on a 'long train journey'. When Jackie told me this I could not make any connection to this, but noted it as Jackie suggested I should. However, a few months later my partner and I booked a holiday abroad to Japan and, surprisingly, he had also booked for both of us to travel on the bullet train in order to see the sights of Japan. This was the train journey Smiley told me about! It was most certainly 'a long train journey', and she was never far from my thoughts.

Smiley clearly is still around watching over me. She had communicated through Jackie so well and it gave me great comfort, knowing that we were never going to be completely apart. I miss her so much, and not a day goes by when I do not think of her.

*****

Truly a life-saver...

Eleanor and her dog TJ

TJ came into my life and the lives of my sons, John and Jason, when he was only eight-weeks-old and that date will be etched in my heart forever.

It was February 17th 1999, John was twelve and Jason was ten. We had been to visit our local cat and dog home in Glasgow looking for a pup. We did see one, but unfortunately it was not possible for us to have it for a while. The boys were disappointed and on the way home I bought the local paper in case there were any pups for sale in it. Later that evening I looked at the pets section and the first advert was for Collie Cross pups for sale at £20 each! I made the phone call straight away and a few hours later, we were to meet the newest member of our family, who would touch all of our hearts.

TJ was a chocolate and white coloured collie cross and we all picked different names for him because of his colour. Suggestions for names were things like Rolo, Choco, etc. but TJ ended up gaining his own name when he helped himself to a tea from a cup placed on the floor! I called him a 'Wee Tea Jenny' and that got abbreviated to TJ and hence his name.

Real Animal Communication Stories No.7

That was very much TJ's character, he thought everything was for him, including the boys' toys. His favourite thing to chew on were the binders of books. We used to joke that it would be disastrous if he was ever left in a library overnight!

As TJ grew, so did the boys. He would be in the bedroom with them as John played with his keyboard and Jason played his video games. If the boys ever got into a play fight, TJ was involved too, not taking sides, but simply enjoying the rough and tumble fun. TJ was there for the boys going to Primary and Secondary school, and for John getting his first job as an apprentice lift engineer, and for Jason, TJ saw him going to college and university, eventually graduating with Honours in Musical Theatre. TJ was always there, supporting our family as it grew.

He was also there for me when I came out of rehab in 2007, at which time TJ was eight-years-old. Anyone who has had to deal with recovery from addiction will know that anyone, or anything, can be your 'Higher Power' for recovery; well TJ was mine. John had moved out to live with his girlfriend, so at home now, it was just Jason, TJ and I. Life was still not easy for any of us all but my 'Higher Power' was still by my side through my weakness and worries, and he gave me the strength and courage to stay strong.

Eventually Jason moved out to live with his partner and it was just TJ and I in the house. Well, he always had been a Mummy's boy anyway, so we were still happy. In December 2012, TJ had what I thought was a chest infection. I took him to the vet and it was discovered that he had problems with his lungs. This was the sort of news I had always been dreading. He was put on steroids and I trawled the internet for information about his condition, looking for ways to

71

help him. I began to buy him oxygen tablets from the local health shop, which actually did seem to help ease his breathing. His walks to the park couldn't be long walks any more as he got tired very easily.

A friend of Jason's offered to let TJ and me stay in her flat, free of charge, for a few days as a retreat after hearing the news, to give us a special break together. She lives on the Island of Millport (off the west coast, not far from Glasgow) so it would be lovely place to stay. I walked TJ along the beach very early in the morning, wondering how long I had left with him. I wished with all my heart that I could turn back time, but my boy was a fighter.

The vets told me I would be lucky to still have TJ come Christmas 2013, but I did still have him and he celebrated his 15th birthday on the 16th December. For Christmas, I got TJ a massive Christmas tree. I went to the pet store and bought him lots and lots of gifts. Christmas was special that year and the boys and their partners came, so the whole family was together. I was able to capture that day on video and will always treasure that Christmas, it means the world to me.

TJ made it into 2014 and was still attending the vet regularly for his lung condition. He was happy in himself and we carried on, but on October 27th I took TJ to the vet as he had been sick multiple times in one week and was going off his favourite treats. Within days, TJ became very slow at walking and was now not finishing off his dinners – he just didn't seem his usual bubbly self. I contacted the vet again, I knew something just wasn't right but assumed he would simply need some antibiotics, which he had had so many times before.

TJ's appointment was for Monday 10th November, 2014, which has become a date I will never forget, as that was the day that broke my heart. The vet who saw TJ this time took a sample of his blood and asked me to wait for the results. Those were the longest forty minutes of my life. I knew in my heart that the news wasn't going to be good and I was right. It was revealed that my wee boy had Chronic Renal Failure. His kidney blood test was reading 24, which was more than double the normal number.

The vet suggested a special food for him, but told me it wouldn't cure him, it would merely slow his deterioration. My faithful, loyal TJ was already having trouble breathing. He was lethargic and feeling weak from not eating enough, but I had to wait and see if this food would help him. I bought some and took TJ home. I bought chicken from the shop and mixed it with this special food and watched with glee as he ate heartily, eating almost all of it. I was over the moon with this development but later that night when he went for a walk, he didn't seem interested. I didn't really sleep that night, I just lay staring at him as he slept, knowing that I had to do what was best for him.

My son John called the next day to ask how TJ was doing. I told him that TJ hadn't eaten that day yet, as well as showing no interest in going outside. John advised me to call the vet back, which I did, and the decision was made to take TJ down there at 5:20pm that evening. I could not comprehend that I had merely a few hours left with my baby boy.

Jason was touring a production out near Aberdeen that week and although he knew that TJ was unwell I couldn't break the news over the phone to him about what was to happen. I called his partner, and asked him if he could do it in my place. Almost instantly, Jason called to reassure me that I was doing the right thing by TJ and not to worry about him not being able to be there. As he couldn't say goodbye in person, he sent TJ through a video message thanking him for always being there, letting him know that he loved him and always would. I showed TJ before we left the house that day. I also thanked him for always being there for the boys and me as they were growing up. Whilst I lay on the bed cuddling him, I played him our song, *You're My World* by Mary Byrne, and I lost count of how many times I told him that I loved him and always would.

John came up straight after his work that day and TJ managed to say hello with a tail wag but didn't get up to greet John as he usually would. John also lay beside him a while petting him before I called a cab to take us to the vet, John rode his work van down to the vet separately.

When TJ was put to sleep, I was on the floor with him repeating over and over that I loved him, and John was petting him. It shattered my heart watching my wee soulmate take his last breath, but I knew in my heart that I was doing the kindest thing possible for him. TJ had always been there for us as a family and now it was our time to repay him by being there for him right to the end. Afterwards, I requested that TJ be individually cremated and returned to me. They told me I could pick him up in a few days' time and that they would be in touch.

John drove me to stay at his house, as going home that night to an empty house was soul destroying. In the days and weeks that followed, I searched the Internet on my Kindle for pet bereavement help, and

I came across a book that Jackie Weaver had written called, *The Voices of Spirit Animals.*

I downloaded it there and then and started reading it that night in bed. After reading a mere few chapters, I got up again and googled Jackie, found her website and was amazed at what I read. I so desperately wanted to get in touch with TJ, to let him know that I did what I did out of love and not because I didn't want him anymore.

I emailed Jackie to enquire about a phone reading and was delighted when she emailed back so quickly, as TJ's 16th birthday was approaching on the 16th and Christmas was coming up. Daniel paid for the phone reading with Jackie, which I had on the 12th of December. It was set for 12pm and as that time approached my eyes were glued to the clock and I had a sick feeling in my stomach, wondering if I would be able to hold it together as the loss still felt very raw.

Jackie called promptly at 12pm and as soon as I heard her voice, I felt such calmness. TJ came through with so much accurate information that it was amazing. He mentioned about feeling so ill that he didn't want to get up. He spoke of being deaf and said that although his eyesight wasn't as good as it had been, he could still see to get around. What really amazed me however was that he said it was fate that had brought him to us, which is true, as I have already explained about the cat and dog home visit. He also spoke about a plant but as I don't keep plants I was confused. I soon remembered that my sister Lorraine had told me she bought a plant recently and had named it TJ! He also described a dog that he used to play with when he was younger but I couldn't place the dog at the time of the reading, however my sons knew of the dog.

He informed Jackie that it was his kidneys that failed him in the end, and also that he had been attending the vets for a while, which was again accurate, due to his earlier lung issues. He also informed her that I had him individually cremated and returned to me.

When Jackie asked if there was anything I wanted to ask TJ, I just wanted to be sure that he knew that I did what I did out of love. She replied that he knew that and that he was aware that I tried very hard to help him ever since he'd become ill, mentioning the blood tests, vet bills and various supplementary medications over the years. He also mentioned that, at the end, nothing could have been done to save him. His kidneys were failing, he said it was simply his time to go. He mentioned he was a family dog who was well loved and in his words, "It was all about the boys!" and that his job was now done, and thanked me for being there for him right to the end. He is right that my world is all about the boys, but he was one of them. In my kitchen I have a notice board and I'd written on it about a year before, "I love my 3 boys" meaning John, Jason and TJ, and on my wrist I got a tattoo saying, "My Boys" for the 3 of them also. I think that was TJ letting me know that he knew I loved him just as much as I did John and Jason.

As the reading was coming to an end, Jackie said although it seemed rather random, she was sure TJ has said "You don't need a new telly!" Now Jackie didn't know what it meant, but I couldn't stop laughing as I knew exactly why TJ was saying that; I had a TV that both my boys thought was outdated and every time they came to my house, they would always say, "You need a new telly!" and when they'd leave, I would sit on the couch with TJ and say to him, "We don't need a new telly TJ, do we?!" I eventually did get a new one before TJ passed but just to hear Jackie say that made me remember such wonderful times with my boy. He said at the end that he was lucky to have me in his life, but I asked Jackie to let him know that we were the lucky ones to have had him in our lives, to share, keep and cherish all the crazy, laughable memories that will live in our hearts forever.

After the reading, I knew 100% that I had done the correct thing. I believe that I wouldn't have coped as well at Christmas, my first without TJ.

Jason, my youngest, suggested that I spend Christmas at his to be away from the house at a time when memories would be a little too raw. Daniel and I travelled with TJ's ashes on Christmas Eve to his house in Glasgow's West End. On Christmas morning, we opened gifts etc. as any family does and then I began to get dressed to go out. I gathered up my things, took TJ's ashes from their place on Jason's fireplace, next to the special glowing angel I had bought for him, and went, on my own, to the park that TJ and I had spent so many beautiful times together over the years. As I entered the park that crisp, frosty morning, I had tears in my eyes though I knew I wasn't alone. Thanks to Jackie's words, I knew I was taking a Christmas morning walk with my beloved TJ in his favourite place. Being able to have this alone time, and knowing that he was with me that day, helped me to make my first Christmas without him physically by my side, be a celebration of his life rather than a mourning of his death. John came up soon after I returned and we had a lovely day and evening full of laughter and joy which would not have been possible without Jackie's reading.

Jackie's gift helped me deal with TJ's passing, and through this, I was in a position to help my friend, James, who had phoned to say that his cat, Frosty, was desperately ill. I met up with him at the vet's surgery which was the same one I had taken TJ to. It was revealed that Frosty was suffering the same kidney issues that TJ had. James made the difficult decision to have Frosty put to sleep but didn't feel strong enough to bear witness to it, so I stepped in and stayed with Frosty as he took his last breath. Such a thing would normally leave me distraught, but through my communications with Jackie, I knew that Frosty would keep in touch with James and that there is a spirit world for not just people, but animals too.

I now know for sure that TJ knows how much he was loved. His passing leaves a void that can never be filled; he was not only a dog, he was a brother, son, confidant and a soulmate. The day he passed away, many hearts were broken. Enjoy your freedom now, TJ, from your aches and pains. We love you to the moon, stars and back again! Mum, John & Jason

*****

Letting Go

Your heart is bursting, searing with pain

That physical touch never to be had again

You only let them go because you so clearly care

They might not be here but they are surely up there.

Real Animal Communication Stories No.7

You feel the pull and the tear of your heart
You feel torn inside and ripped apart
The enormity of choosing what best to do
It was done with your love, as they looked to you.

We don't enter into this without thought or care
We do it because the compassion is there
The choice to stop pain and distress of the one we love
Can only be guided by you and the angels above.

Many spirits have come through and given me their word
Your tears of sorrow and distress they heard
But they are free and happy and hold no ill will
Whatever was wrong could not have been cured with a pill.

The height of pain is a measuring device
It shows how deeply you felt throughout their life
With your love given for this most selfless act
They at least left this earth with their heart intact.

Now up yonder and free to roam
This is another level, like a new home
The day will come when you go up there too
They're ready and waiting to meet and embrace you.

Jackie Weaver

If you truly did this from your genuine heart
You were so brave and helped them depart
Your love and courage was seen from above
This really was your strongest act of love.

If you could ask them now, what might they say?
"In my life, that was actually only one single day,
Please remember the rest, the joy, love and play,
For I look down from above and remember it that way."

As time has passed you may at last feel some ease
Maybe a pet has come for you to please
Animals are not selfish and want you to share
They left that space for another needing your love and care.

We are truly honoured to share in their space
Think back and let that smile adorn your face
The precious time you had could never be measured
Your lasting memories are of those you truly treasured.

Jackie Weaver 2009

*****

Real Animal Communication Stories No.7

Such a proud gentleman...

Rosemary and her dog Jasper

I totally believe that animals come into one's life for a purpose and that they are great teachers, Jasper my beautiful black Labrador is no exception. He is my unplanned baby who arrived on the doorstep at only nine weeks old, a gift from a lovely lady who felt she could not cope with a puppy at a difficult time in her life. Jasper came straight in and made himself at home and we have never looked back! The adventure had begun...

Initially we did nine months of basic obedience then one day, I noticed that most of the names on his pedigree were marked in red with 'F.T. CH.' after them. I made enquiries and was told that this referred to gundog 'Field Trial Champion'. So began our years of training and competing Gundog Working Tests, which resulted in Jasper being known as the 'black panther' due to his amazingly sensitive nose! He was well known for jumping five barred gates complete with pheasant held in his jaw! One glorious day we won through from Novice to Open status and received an amazing silver shield leaving me totally speechless. (A hitherto, unknown phenomenon!) In the meantime Jasper was excelling at Agility and we began competing whenever we could, achieving a wall full of rosettes and reaching level 2 last year.

Just for fun a few years ago I entered him in a large pedigree show and to our total surprise Jasper walked away with not only the silver cup for 'Best Gundog' but also a huge silver trophy for 'Best in Show Pedigree'. I have never been so proud of my all round superstar! Now we are perfecting his tricks, 'Hi Fives' to my salute, jumping over my leg and through hand held hoops, rolling over, weaving through my legs in a figure of eight, lying still with biscuits on his head and paws whilst other biscuits are dropped around him, shaking to command after swimming, to name but a few.

Jasper is my life; we do everything together and he understands everything I say but I desperately needed to know his side of the arrangement, what he thought, what he liked, and disliked, and changes that could be made to improve his life! This is where Jackie came in and totally changed things for us both. By 'coincidence' (I believe there is no such thing), I heard that Jackie would be attending *The Healing Weekend* in Somerset. I made certain that Jasper and I were first in the queue and the results were astounding! Throughout the session Jasper lay by my feet watching people and dogs walking past yet his subconscious mind chattered away 'ninety to the dozen'.

Jasper said he liked to be alone at times, likes the car and would appreciate longer walks – he would walk all day, every day, I am sure! He then tells Jackie that I make him look at water! This is so true because he leaps a long distance in and I want time to check if there are branches under the water that would injure him. I am glad he understands, clever boy.

Jackie says he comes across as very stoic but mentions a bit of tartar or gingivitis on right side of mouth. I was able to confirm this immediately without looking as I had already massaged his gum a few days ago thinking there was something amiss!

He says he is very intelligent, he understands what I say to him. He loves hugs and praise means a lot to him. He is, 'Good with the GIRLS!' This made me smile as he does like the girls as he is a 'daddy' and I

Real Animal Communication Stories No.7

am sure is keen to keep up the good work. A litter of his pups had been born not long ago and I am delighted to say that I am having one so thought this was a good point to ask Jackie what his opinion was about the whole thing. As I thought, he was absolutely fine and said he would like to look after our new pup but would like a break from it at times! (I had already thought of that and made an agreement with him.)

He says his eyesight is okay and that it is his best feature. Jackie then told me about a clever, and very personal idea she has come up with which is actually being able to put the owner into the eyes of their pet, like a reflection would be. I immediately asked her to do one for me. I had to send a decent sized photo of his head, eyes forward, and then one of me that she could use to put in his eyes. Whilst having our reading, a dog came too close to Jasper at Jackie's stall, so Jasper growled. I was quite surprised but then said, "That was to the owners not the dogs!" Jackie agreed too I had to agree with them both as why do people just let their dogs, even though they are on a lead, just do what they want in regards to approaching other dogs? In my book, if my dog is on a lead then he is under control and may not like (be scared of) other dogs for various reason, so surely people could learn to respect that instead of letting them approach regardless of any consequences on either side.

Jasper said he was a proud dog and then the word 'Silver'. I am sure this referred to the huge silver cup for Best in Show Pedigree, his silver shield for winning into Open Gundog trials, a silver agility cup and a silver best gundog trophy – lots of silver! Jasper says many people want him. Oh yes, and if I had a pound for every time it was said as it is such a long, and ever increasing list, of everyone who gets to know him! He is of a 'good stamp' not the whippet sort. He would like more food when breeding and said 'raw' is good for the enzymes. (I have now put him on raw food plus his dog biscuits). He mentioned his poo's at that point, and I have to say, with the slight change of diet, look a lot healthier now! He enjoys food with great smells so now when camping, as a treat, I cook a bacon rasher for him! Jasper said he could have been a guide dog and would like to be a PAT dog when he is ten years old. That would be just so lovely and he would be wonderful at it. He then declared that 'matings will make money.' (Within half an hour of that talk I received the first of three enquiries for mating Jasper from stallholders!)

I mentioned about his fear of thunder and Jackie advised him not to fear the thunder as it is outside and cannot come inside his house and will not harm him. She expressed to him that I will never allow any harm to come to him. Jasper says thunder means 'bacon!' Well he is so switched on as Jackie had quickly asked if anything could make him feel better about the thunder, and there was his answer. Talk about a negative to a positive! Talking about his house, he kindly volunteered that there was a picture that is hanging crooked in the house. I had to laugh as this is so true and actually is a picture I painted of Jasper as a pup. The hook on the frame was not central but... since his chat, it has since been reframed in a grander style of frame, and hangs perfectly too! He then 'lowered the tone' by volunteering that he has a bladder like a tank! He has! I was telling Jackie that he pees for minutes on end and I have never known a dog like it. Unbelievably he then still marks every tree and scent

Real Animal Communication Stories No.7

he passes and with that, Jasper interjected that that was a 'different type of Pee!'

Jasper says that he is at peace with his life and trusts me to look after him, he has no worries and knows he is at the centre of my life and all that I do. Jasper says we do not need to learn telepathy as we are doing it anyway and we are the special ones.

This communication has been the 'icing on the cake' for our relationship as Jasper and I now work even closer together. My life has also changed as I have decided to follow my passion for understanding and helping animals, with Jasper and I working closely as a pair. I know he will be fine with the pup and a good father figure to him. I give thanks for my wonderful companion every moment of every day. Jasper 'ticks every box' for me he is extremely handsome, a real gentleman, great fun, exceptionally good-natured with the most amazing eyes. As for evenings... sorry I am unable to answer the door or the telephone, as I will be pinned in my chair with my darling Jasper curled up asleep in my arms and cannot be disturbed!

Thank you Jackie and Jasper for a wonderful half an hour of communication that has now added yet another dimension to our already beautiful life.

*****

Coming to a good understanding...

Sara and her horse Milly

My name is Sara and I am 47 years old. I have had ponies and horses all of my life and I am able to forge close relationships with those that will allow this. As a child my ponies were always naughty and by the age of ten I point blankly refused to ride any more naughty ponies, and in the end I rode my Mum's little horse instead.

Over time I have learnt that every horse is different: some will welcome love and cuddles, while others will keep a cool distance. Some can't wait to see you with a warm greeting, whilst others seem to have that look of, 'Don't bother, I'm off'. I once had a horse called Rocky that would take a chunk out of everyone that walked past his door. No one could catch him out in the field, as he would greet you with up coming front feet and a wide-open mouth! Yet Rocky and I were the best of friends, and I could catch him and do anything with him. He was the 'he man' of the yard and couldn't get enough work, so I rode him every day and worked him really hard and he thrived on it. We won lots of events and he will always be a legend for his antics.

I have been lucky enough to have some very special and talented horses. One horse, Spikey, was stunning. A chestnut boy with the most beautiful white blaze and white socks, and he qualified four years on the trot for the Working Hunter at Horse of the Year Show, and he was placed at it too! He was naughty to start with, but oh so bold, and we forged a special relationship, understanding each other completely. I had him from a foal but sadly he died at the age of twenty four. I can't spend enough time with horses and enjoy breaking them in and starting their careers off – even after a couple of broken noses and lots of blood, sweat and tears, I would get there in the end whatever issues they might have been having.

I was very lucky to have been left some money from my godmother I never knew she was going to do this and feel touched that she did, but also sad that I could never thank her. I did nothing with this money for a long time but one day a friend phoned and said, "Come down and see what I've got." So I duly drove for over an hour to get to this friend's house but had I known I was going to view a grey mare then I would never have left home, let alone a grey Warmblood mare. Nothing against greys or Warmbloods, but they would never have been my first choice.

So I looked at this horse and then stood in the stable with her for about 20 minutes. I don't know if it was vibes, but there certainly was an immediate connection and intrigue. I asked to ride her and popped some jumps with her. It was like fatal attraction. At the end of the week I went and collected Milly, who was looking like a hyped up lunatic! I said I would have her for a week and I would see how it stands again. She actually settled well but had this flight or fight streak. When scared or unsure of how to react and deal with a situation, she would go vertical. People would look aghast when this happened, but I just ignored her and rode on although, I admit, inside me I just wanted to leap off.

I struggled with Milly and couldn't find any bit that she was happy with in her mouth. She would go flat out eventing and it was a constant battle to have brakes or steering at times. I tried literally hundreds. I was then at an event and spoke with a friend, Sue, who runs an equestrian shop. I said to her, "I have come to the end of the road with Milly and don't know where to go." She said that if I was interested and into 'that sort of thing' she would give me the name of lady that could maybe help. My reply was that I would try anything for Milly to let me know what the problem was.

So I was given the name of Jackie Weaver. I thought, "Well I have nothing to lose here and hopefully everything to gain." I sent a photo of Milly's face to Jackie and a phone call took place. The conversation started with Milly telling Jackie that she was not for sale. Phah, she nearly was, and many times, I can tell you! But quite right, she is with me for life. She said she is exuberant and most extravagant in her movement – this Milly certainly is. She is stunning and a real eye catcher and so many people have stopped and said, "Just look at her" or, "oh isn't she beautiful." But how on earth could Jackie tell me that by looking at a photo of nothing but her head? How could she tell me Milly loved being watched and looking pretty? Milly likes nothing more than being centre of attention. She said that she was agile and had loads of scope, which led us to the most interesting part of the conversation, regarding her lightning speed when doing cross-country competitions. I explained to Jackie that I constantly tell Milly when we are travelling fast towards some big cross country fences that she needs to listen to ME, as I have walked the course and know what's coming!

The response from Milly made me laugh. She said, "Mum, just sit up and balance me, use your legs and less hand to steer me. I like that!" She went on to explain to Jackie that she has a sore bit in her mouth and her tongue also gets squashed up, and that is why she fights and throws her head up at me. Bingo! Problem solved – I now have a bit that is shaped to allow her tongue room and yes, I do sit up and balance her, laughing all the way now. Milly then made a statement that made me cry. "Whatever happens Mum, I will always look after you." What a

Real Animal Communication Stories No.7

statement to come from this 'lunatic' that came to me, and now who now cannot get enough kisses and cuddles. Boy, when she wants a cuddle she will get one, without a doubt. Her face is in mine and she loves kisses on the bottom of her ears. She nuzzles my neck and lets me know unreservedly that she loves me too.

We had issues with dressage too, but Milly told Jackie that she really is not that keen on doing it and just wants to get on and get it over with! Just like the dentist I suppose, necessary but not nice. So Jackie made an agreement with Milly (at the same time stating that she could not promise it would work) that I would sit and transfer the thought, "This is important." I tried this and guess what? We were placed 3rd in our next big one-day event. I laughed all the way around the cross-country, saying to Milly, "Is this balanced enough madam for you?" It really helped us both riding her the way she wanted and she did listen, well most of the time. Spectators must have thought I was mad, laughing and talking to her, but now I know that we can understand each other life is really good.

Milly also told Jackie about a scar and accident she had when she was young, galloping into something. She said her scar is unique and she is very stoical about it. Again, how on earth could Jackie know this? Jackie has such a special gift and talent to be able to communicate with animals. During our phone conversation I laughed, concentrated, and cried. Such emotion hearing what my beautiful talented horse had to say, especially as at one point as she really had driven me to despair. I can't thank Jackie enough and have talked about it with so many people I have met.

You are special Jackie, and thank you very, very much for helping Milly and me.

*****

Such a brave and wonderful little dog...

Michelle and her dog Ziggy

I remember going to choose my little Yorkie puppy. I had read all the books and decided a little boy would suit me best, but as soon as I saw the ball of black and ginger fluff relaxing behind her squabbling siblings, I just knew it didn't matter what sex she was - we were meant to be together. My little 'boy' Yorkshire Terrier was now a 'girl' and I christened her Ziggy.

I was so right – from that moment on she and I were inseparable. I took her everywhere with me. When I look back at photos now that are supposed to be just of me, it warms my heart to see my little dog, Ziggy, always somewhere in a corner, or just off to the side of me. We were so inseparable that she would even sit on my lap when I was having my hair cut!

Although she was only a little dog she had such a big personality; she was always making people laugh with her funny little ways yet, at the same time, she was content for us to find a quiet spot in the countryside, sit on my lap, and watch the world go by. Often she would doze off and I just loved those precious times we shared, just us together.

We were so close that she always knew if I was upset or sad; she would snuggle down next to me and let me bury my face in her warm fur until I felt better. She not only helped me through so many hard times in my life, but she also helped others as well. I remember my parents' little dog Charlie had been

Real Animal Communication Stories No.7

attacked by three dogs and since then had wanted nothing to do with any other dogs, and understandably so. Slowly but surely, Ziggy and Charlie became lifelong friends and she taught him to play again.

Virtually from the beginning, Ziggy had battled with a heart murmur and a skin condition. Although, saying that, she had always seemed happy and healthy, but then after her fifth birthday the problems began.

The first thing I noticed was an increase in her drinking and although I tried different foods, thinking maybe they were wrong for her, nothing reduced it. I really became concerned when I noticed she seemed to be losing weight too. The vet confirmed my worst fears; although her usual bright self, Ziggy was actually very ill. She had diabetes and ketones in her urine. (With the lack of insulin, the body cannot burn sugar so it will burn stored fat and ketones are a dangerous result of this.) They took her straight into hospital where she stayed for ten days while they tried to stabilise her diabetes. In the end, a lovely vet who took on Ziggy's case, told us it was more down to Ziggy now and whether she had the willpower to pull herself through or not. I, or my family, visited her every day and little by little she started to get better. Eventually, we brought her home, complete with loads of insulin injections that she now needed twice a day.

I was determined that no matter what it cost I was going to get Ziggy as well as possible and, even though people said to me that she might not live to a grand old age, I would not accept that would be the case. For a while she did pick up, it was like having the old happy healthy Ziggy back again. However, on a routine check up it was found that due to her diabetes her kidneys had now become damaged. Her diabetes was such a difficult case to keep under control that, even at that stage, she was still not responding to the insulin exactly as the vet would have liked but, as Ziggy appeared so happy and healthy, she began treatment to support her kidneys. Also, as if things were not tough enough, we noticed she had started to lose her sight and the vet confirmed she now had cataracts. They said she could still see but her vision would be very misty.

Even with failing eyesight, she still didn't let this get in her way and for two years, she seemed happy and full of life. As long as the furniture at home was kept in the same place, and she went to her favourite fields for walks, she would run around like she was still a puppy whilst I made sure I was her guide so that she didn't bump into anything and hurt herself.

She had made it to seven-years-old and then one day, for no apparent reason, she started to go off her food. We tried all of her favourite things to encourage her, and at first it worked. With the worst timing possible, I had to go in to have an operation. The next day, when my husband visited, he told me that when he had woken up that morning, Ziggy had not greeted him with her usual little howl of joy and that she hadn't eaten a thing. Back to the Vet hospital she went and then, after more tests, they phoned to say she was very ill again but from another condition called Addison's disease. This was such bad news, as it had made her diabetes even more unstable, but they would keep her there and do all they could to save her.

I felt so helpless because, although I was now out of hospital, the doctor had put me on bed rest so I

Real Animal Communication Stories No.7

couldn't even go to be with her. On the third day I got the most devastating phone call, Ziggy had taken a turn for the worst and she was now in pain – it was so devastating to hear this. All the times that my little one had been there for me when I had cried, I now couldn't get to her when she needed me most. My heart broke when the vet said there was nothing more she could do for Ziggy. I knew I had to be strong for her, so I made the decision to bring her home to have her put to sleep here with us. She was given a very high dose of painkiller and she was collected. I do think she knew she was at home again with me. I had forty five minutes before the vet was due to arrive so I held her close telling her how much I loved her and how special she was. Whilst holding her in my arms, the vet gave Ziggy her last injection and she went peacefully to sleep for the last time.

I cannot describe the devastation I felt afterwards – she had been such a huge part of my life. There were reminders of her everywhere. Even now as I write this, I still find myself thinking it can't be true that I will never again see her sitting on the bottom stair waiting for me to come down, or feel her little paw rapping on my leg gently to be picked up.

I felt I desperately wanted to know: where was she? Was she happy? Was it my fault? Could I have done something differently? So I started to look for animal psychics on the internet. I found many different names, but the one that kept coming up was Jackie's. There were so many wonderful testimonials from people who had spoken to her that I knew I had to contact her.

On the day of my reading I was so nervous; I counted down the minutes until our arranged time and yet, when Jackie called, she instantly put me at ease and came across as such a genuine, down to earth person. She knew so many things about Ziggy and me that I knew she had to be communicating with Ziggy.

Jackie told me that although many dogs did not like their feet to be touched, I had stroked her paws and she had loved this. This was so true; Ziggy would even lie down and give me her paw to massage. Jackie then asked if she used to lie next to my head on the pillow. This was exactly right, she did! Right from when she was a puppy, with the best of intentions, I'd settle her in her own little bed, but would always wake up to find her snuggled into me on my pillow.

Jackie told me how Ziggy had been a fun dog, jumping up and down excitedly. We would always laugh or smile when she did as, whenever she would meet people she knew and loved, she would jump up and down on her hind legs making little happy howling noises.

I was amazed when Jackie said it seemed that Ziggy had on-going illnesses, but that she had not let it stand in her way and it had been manageable until the end. Jackie even knew that Ziggy drank a lot due to her illness (which is a sign of diabetes) and that it appeared to her as if Ziggy was looking through net curtains. I knew this must be how it had appeared to her when she developed cataracts.

Jackie helped me so much when she said she knew that I had felt so much guilt over everything that had happened, but that Ziggy was telling her I had nothing to feel guilty about. Ziggy said that I had given her so much love and a wonderful life and that she was going to get ill no matter what because she had 'a poor system' as she put it. When I think about

Real Animal Communication Stories No.7

it, from such an early stage of her life she had always had one problem or another.

I asked Jackie about Ziggy and my husband, as we had met two years after I first got her and she had always taken a while to get to know new people. Jackie said that although Ziggy was definitely my dog she had loved my husband very much and that he was a very straightforward, genuine man, which he is. Jackie amazed me when she said, "As I talk about him, I see him with a big black dog. Would that be significant to him?" Yes it certainly was!

When Ziggy was three years old we had adopted a Rottweiler puppy called Echo. We always enjoyed people's reactions to the size difference: little and large. Jackie said that although Echo was obviously physically much bigger than Ziggy, this was never a problem, as they seemed to get on very well together. They most certainly did – they adored each other. Ziggy said to remember that I can speak to her because she will still hear me. Now I truly know that she is living in spirit, I most definitely will.

Ziggy told Jackie that everyone at the vets knew her by her first name and that they were so kind to her and expressed that she was an 'unfortunate soul.' She had such a lovely, gentle and fun personality, that many of the veterinary staff said she was one of their favourites. Ziggy also suggested if there wasn't already a book of condolences at the surgery, maybe I should suggest it. Jackie was amazed at such a wonderful idea and said that it would be such a touching thing for all vet practices to have. She thought that vets would also be very moved by the lovely notes that grateful owners had written on behalf of their pets, as much as the owners would be to be able to leave their pet's name in writing there. I had to agree – what a beautiful idea and it would have been so typical of my little girl.

The thing that gave me the most hope for the future was when Jackie asked me if I had ever thought about fostering dogs? She said Ziggy was telling her I should be very proud of all I had done and that I had learned so much from looking after her. Yes, it had been a hard road but I could use all I had learned to care for other dogs with disabilities. It was so strange (although not so much now I know that they do watch over us) because only the day before I had decided just that!

From now on, every dog I took in, would be a dog that perhaps other people might not be able able to take on due to their disability. I knew from Ziggy that, by having problems and needing special care, served only to make them even more special and I would do my utmost to give them the best quality of life as possible. So, in Ziggy's memory, I will do this.

I cannot thank Jackie enough. Her messages from Ziggy made such an impact on me and helped me through the heartbreak of losing her but at least, thanks to this communication, I know we will most definitely be together again one day.

*****

Real Animal Communication Stories No.7

The boy who eventually became ours…

Lesley and her cat Sox

Sox first came to us in 2009, though we did not adopt him until 2010. He was a tabby cat but, as the name suggests, he had white fur on all four paws.

Sox turned up one morning in January 2009, watching us from the garden fence. He looked well fed and healthy, so we assumed that he belonged to a neighbour and did not pay much attention to him for the first 12 months. He would visit regularly, keeping his distance by sitting on the fence at the end of the garden and watching us curiously with our three cats. He would occasionally disappear for a few weeks, but always came back to see us. In March 2010 Sox disappeared once more and we did not see him again until he returned in June that year.

During this time, one of our other cats became seriously ill and passed over. A few weeks later we saw an online ad placed by the RSPCA, which was an urgent appeal to rehome a black male cat called Casper. Casper had spent several months in a foster home, as the RSPCA were struggling to rehome him; they told us it was because no one wanted black cats due to superstition. Casper was two years old, very timid and scared of everything. We went to see him at his foster home and decided immediately that we would adopt him. Since Casper was so nervous we decided not to take in any more cats, so as not to upset him… then Sox turned up!

This time we noticed Sox had lost a lot of weight; he was so thin that we could see his ribs. He was also very weak and struggled to climb over the fence. We tried to get him to come to us but he did not want to come, and so started to put food out for him and

97

made him a bed in the garden shed. Over the next few days we managed to get him to come closer and closer to us until eventually he decided to come for a stroke. He was very friendly and trusted us immediately. However, he did not get on with other cats and we thought we would have a problem with him if we took him in. We tried to find out if he belonged to anyone and when he trusted us enough for us to pick him up, we took him to the vets to check for a microchip, but he did not have one.

When the vet examined him he told us that whoever Sox belonged to, they had not looked after him very well as he was not neutered and had worms and fleas. As he was a stray we had no idea of his exact age but the vet said he was around five to six years old. We took him home and continued to feed him while we searched for his owners. We asked neighbours and looked online for lost pets, but had no luck. After about three months we contacted The Cats Protection to ask for advice, they sent us a paper collar on which we could put our phone number so that his owners could contact us. When it arrived we put the collar on him and let him out. The next day he turned up again but without the collar. When no one called us we decided it was time to get him neutered. We hoped that it would stop him wandering off for weeks on end and also calm him down a bit with other cats. It did stop him wandering and he began spending more time in the garden with us, but he still did not get on with other cats.

Over the next few months we managed to get him to come into the porch, and then the kitchen for his food, but as soon as he had finished he would go back out again. Eventually he started to go upstairs and sleep in one of the cat beds on the landing, and

Real Animal Communication Stories No.7

then slowly over a few more weeks he moved into the bedroom and onto the bed.

As our other cat Casper was very nervous and fearful – and Sox by this time had grown into a strong and very solid cat, (he loved his food and had a belly to prove it), Casper was scared of him and would run away. He would hide under the wardrobe and anywhere else he could find that made him feel safe. If they were both out at the same time, Casper would not come home until he was sure Sox was not around. So, the only solution was to keep them separated. This was difficult at first but gradually we got into a routine with them.

We soon discovered that Sox liked to be out at night and spend the day sleeping on the bed, while Casper and our other two cats preferred to be out during the day. After we got to know Sox a little better we realised that he was more of an outdoor cat, preferring his own company to that of others and doing his own thing. However, he always liked to know that we were there when he needed us, particularly at meal times. Sox loved to be fussed, but on his terms, and he had one of the loudest and deepest meows and purrs we have ever heard. If another cat came into the garden he would chase them off; he was very territorial and we put this down to him not being neutered when he was younger. After he was neutered he did calm down a bit, particularly in the last couple of years of his life, but still had issues with other cats, nevertheless. He was very friendly and loving with people he knew, but did not like strangers.

Sox's daily routine was to spend the night out – either hunting or guarding his territory, and sleeping in his own bedroom that we made for him in the garden shed. In winter we put heat pads in his bed for him to keep him warm, which he liked very much as we had difficulty moving him off them. Every morning he would be waiting at the back door for his breakfast, he would come running in to eat his food then make a dash upstairs into the bedroom, jump on the table, and spend the next few minutes looking out of the window, watching people going to work or walking their dogs. Occasionally he would catch a glance of Casper running down the drive and this would set his tail wagging wildly. Finally, when he was feeling sleepy he would climb on to the bed and settle down, with his head on a cushion, for the rest of the day.

In the afternoon he liked to go out for a few hours, mainly sitting in the garden, watching the birds and squirrels argue over food, or he would go over the fence to play in the field. Every now and again we would hear caterwauling and knew immediately that it was Sox arguing with the neighbours' cats. Sometimes he would come over the fence looking a bit defeated. He never went far away from his home, as when we shouted him, a minute or so later he would be back in the garden. In the evening he would come in for his tea, followed by some treats of fresh chicken or tuna and then have a few hours sleep in his bed on the landing before going out again for the night. We tried to get him to stay in but he always wanted to go out at the same time every night, he would sit at the back door looking eager to get out. He would not play with cat toys, but we discovered that he loved catnip and playing with laser lights, chasing around trying to catch the light.

This routine went on for six years, until 3 May 2016 when sadly we had to have Sox put to sleep. It came

Real Animal Communication Stories No.7

as a shock to us all as seven days earlier he seemed fine. One Sunday lunchtime we noticed he was limping, yet the day before he seemed fine. He was sat in the garden enjoying the sun and came in for his food as usual and we thought he might have injured his paw while he was out the night before. When we examined his paws we could not see anything. We booked him in to see the vet the next day, they examined him and said they could not find anything wrong with him. The vet told us the limping could be due to arthritis and prescribed him Metacam. We went away and started Sox on the Metacam, but three days later his limping became worse rather than better. He was finding it difficult to jump and climb the stairs, so we took him back to the vets and told them we wanted tests done on him. They were reluctant to do them at first as they thought we had not given the Metacam long enough to work. They were still adamant that it was arthritis as he had no other symptoms but we were doubtful about this diagnosis. We finally managed to get them to book him in for tests, but had to wait another three days. By that time Sox had deteriorated; he could not walk at all and was dragging his legs across the floor.

On the Friday morning we took Sox to the vets as arranged and they did a blood test on him. It showed a problem with his kidneys, but the vet informed us that this might have been caused by an infection and would clear up on its own if this was the case. They told us to stop the Metacam immediately as this irritated the kidneys, and instead they gave him medication for his kidneys and painkillers, in case he was in any pain. Nevertheless, his back legs were continuing to get worse, they were growing cold and colder, and seemed he could not feel anything. By this stage Sox could no longer go outside and this was making him miserable.

Over the next couple of days we struggled to get Sox to have the medication, we crushed the tablets up and put them in his favourite treats of chicken and tuna, but he could smell the medication in it and would not touch it. We mixed it in his cat food but to not avail. Finally we tried to put them straight down his throat, but he would fight us and when we did get them down, he regurgitated them. We ended up having to take him to the vets for them to administer the medication. By this time though he had stopped eating and drinking. The vet was concerned about this and examined him once again. He informed us that Sox was in a very bad way, he had lost the feeling in his back legs and they told us he would never get it back, and because of this he could not empty his bladder which was making him uncomfortable.

The vet advised that the kindest thing to do was have him put to sleep and reluctantly we agreed. It was never explained to us what happened to his back legs, and moreover, we have had cats in the past with kidney disease and knew the symptoms to look out for. Sox did not show any visible symptoms of kidney problems – his coat was in excellent condition, he was not over drinking water, he had lost some weight, but that was on the advice of the vet the year before and not because of illness, so we were left not knowing what really went wrong with Sox.

I have always believed in the spirit world and know that they send us signs and messages in various ways. An hour after Sox was put to sleep a large white feather floated down in front of the car while we were stopped at traffic lights; we took this as a sign

Real Animal Communication Stories No.7

from Sox that he had arrived safely and he was well again. The day after Sox passed over I Googled animal psychics and Jackie's name was at the top of the list. I contacted Jackie to see if she could shed some light on what went wrong with Sox's back legs. I knew it was not arthritis as it came on too suddenly and thought there was something more to it. I have had several readings in the past from other psychics, but not for animals, and I had no doubt about Jackie's abilities. I emailed Jackie giving her my name, his name, age and when he passed along with a photograph of him too.

Jackie telephoned me and explained to me that it was a three-way conversation between herself, Sox and me. During the conversation Jackie provided information that only Sox would know, and as soon as she spoke to me I knew that she had made contact with Sox. Jackie described him as a strong, but gentle cat that enjoyed his own company and was very independent. Sox told Jackie that we let him come to us, which was correct; we let Sox decide if he wanted to live with us, we did not force him to move in. We realised he had spent a lot of time outdoors before coming to us and did not want to upset him by forcing him to live with us. Sox gave further confirmation that it was him by showing Jackie a black cat rolling over, which was Casper.

More information followed that Jackie could not possibly have known. In particular, she described Sox as a cat that did not like fighting, as he knew he would lose. At first I thought this did not sound like Sox, he was well known for not getting on with other cats. As he got older though, and more settled in our home, he did seem to avoid other cats and only occasionally argued with them if they came in the garden, even then he would come in the house looking a bit fed up and dishevelled, Sox did think he was the boss of all other cats. We did not know why Sox was like this and used to joke by saying that Sox was a bit of a bully, but Sox told Jackie that he was authoritative and not a bully! Jackie explained to me the reason for this behaviour was that Sox was showing her that he was kicked out of one home and did not want to lose another. He apologised about his reaction to other cats and said now that he is in spirit, he could try to help Casper to be braver.

Jackie went on to describe to me a feeling of bloating in the abdomen and a progressive illness that was irreversible. I told her that Sox had been given Metacam for arthritis, and she explained to me that she had come across many cases where Metacam had caused stomach upsets, and cramps put animals off their food. Sox acknowledged that he was up and moving about the day before, then something happened with his lower spine, some sort of constriction – his legs and lower back became weak and he was dragging himself across the floor, which described his symptoms exactly and related to the loss of feeling in his legs. This information Jackie gave me confirmed for me that it was not arthritis. What she was saying about something happening in his lower back spine area caused the loss of sensation of the backend thus not being able to urinate. Sox said that he could not have gone on and wanted us to know that we made the right decision. We would not want him to wallow in self-pity and he did not want to lose his independence. However, he was keen to point out that 'the birds will miss him', which is true, he liked to watch the birds in the garden – he never went after them, he would just sit and watch them from the steps – and had become quite friendly towards them.

Jackie described him sitting on the fence watching and sitting upright at a door. He was always sitting on the fence, both watching our neighbours and looking into the field. The 'upright' description was exactly how he would sit at the back door when he wanted to go out at night. She said that he did not go far, which was correct; after we took him in, he was happy to spend most of his time in the garden and field at the back of the house.

Jackie mentioned a crystal in a window reflecting light. There is a crystal sun catcher in the window of the bedroom in which Sox liked to sleep in during the day, I have had this for 20 years, and when the light catches it, it cast a rainbow on the walls. Sox told Jackie that when it caught the light, to think of him as he had mentioned it.

I had to laugh when Jackie went on to describe what she saw as a light. She laughingly said, "For want of a better description, it looked something resembling a UFO going round!" At first I could not relate to this but then it clicked; I identified it the ceiling fan in the upstairs bedroom, which has a light on it! Sox was very familiar with this fan as he loved to lie under it in summer, he would lie on his back watching it spinning round. Jackie was also correct when she said that Sox did not sleep on the bed at night, she had no idea that Sox was out at night, and this was the reason why he did not come on the bed.

Sox also remembered the laser light that he loved to play with as Jackie went on to describe Sox watching something, she described it as a light flashing or some sort of game that he was watching. I told Jackie that it is a laser light pen with a red beam, it is attached to a keyring and I discovered, by accident, that both Sox and Casper liked to chase the light around the room. When Sox heard the keyring jingle against the pen, his ears would prick up as he used to recognise the sound immediately and want to play with it. He was playing with it a couple of days before he passed over, although he could not use his back legs his front paws were fine and he was very alert. Jackie said that Sox wants us to think of him like this when he was playing and not how he was when he was ill.

Jackie also described a white cat with Sox, she said that the cat was a bit scruffy and dirty looking. I identified the cat as Smudge, one of our other cats that passed over in 2013 aged 19 years old. Smudge had always been a very clean cat so at first I could not relate to it, but then I remembered that because of his age Smudge's fur, particularly around his paws, had started to go a bit dirty towards the end of his life and this would account for the description… Sox, was eager to point out that he kept himself clean, which was very true.

Jackie told me that Sox was showing her something being scattered or thrown in the garden. A couple of days after Sox passed over I began throwing birdseed and peanuts on the ground for the birds, which I have never done before. I usually place the food on the bird table, and Jackie informed me that Sox was watching me do this. Sox was also aware of us saying that we were missing him. Jackie told me that Sox said he had moved in and never moved out, and that he felt safe with us and had no regrets.

After my conversation with Jackie I felt much better knowing that we had done the right thing. I let my parents read the notes I made, and they were very impressed with our conversation. They, like me, are

Real Animal Communication Stories No.7

totally convinced that Sox is still around in spirit watching over us all. Thank you very much Jackie.

*****

The boy that actually knew more...

Rachael and her dog Frank

We decided after the death of our dog Harvey that we were going to get two dogs. They were both going to be rescues, so off we went to see which dogs our local shelter had. When we arrived we were immediately drawn to Buster. All of our previous 'big' dogs were black Labradors and Buster looked like he had some lab in there, and he was black, just the type we were looking for. Sharing the kennel with him was Frank who was a handsome Saluki cross and unlike any type of dog we had had before. I'll come back to this point later as it came up in my reading with Jackie but, as we wanted two dogs, we thought we would take Frank along with Buster.

We had our home check and after a week or so we went to pick up the dogs. Frank was straight into the car, however, Buster was a different matter; I had to half drag, half lift him in and he managed to chew through his new lead on the way home!

Then began the task of settling in our two new arrivals... Buster was one-year-old and full of life, but Frank seemed to be such a sad boy. He was four and, from what we could gather, had been in the shelter for nearly a year. Apparently he was initially a stray, but his owner was found and they took him home, but then returned him back to the shelter! He didn't seem to know how to play and just looked generally sorry for himself. We soon set about making him at home and he loved being in our

107

company and sitting with you (or frequently on top of you!) on the sofa.

Gradually Frank began to relax and his sad expression soon changed into a cheeky happy one. Frank was always up to something! He was the most intelligent dog I have ever known and when I left home to work elsewhere my mum would relay the latest tales of what the dogs had been up to. This would usually involve some 'incident' or another, with Frank looking innocent and Buster getting the blame.

One classic example of this was the case of the missing mince pie. You could not leave an open bag anywhere on the floor in the house as Frank would have his whole head in there before you knew it. We warned visitors about this constantly, but warnings were not always heeded. On this occasion one of my dad's carers had just been to the butchers for a mince pie and left the bag on the floor. Needless to say when she came to leave there was no mince pie and after a short search Buster was found licking a small remnant of the tin foil that held the pie. I had warned Mum that Frank was very clever and good at looking innocent but she told me that Buster had duly been told off. Lo and behold, later that day, who vomited up the mince pie complete with most of the tin foil but Frank!

Buster eventually got used to the car and Frank and Buster's relationship in terms of the car was so funny; Frank would line up first eager to get in, but would take so long to get in with his long limbs that Buster would barge past and be on the seat first!

Our lives continued with lots of happy times with the dogs for many years. This all abruptly came to an end

Real Animal Communication Stories No.7

when one morning my brother was drying Frank off after his walk and discovered a huge lump on his side. It was as if it had appeared from nowhere. We all hoped that it was just an abscess but the vet looked worried. They x-rayed and it was a tumour that had been growing inside Frank and had eventually popped out. By the time it had appeared it was too late to do anything. We were devastated as Frank had been fine up to then, it was very hard to accept. The vet put Frank on steroids and some painkillers and we kept him at home until he started showing symptoms of pain. We knew we didn't want him to suffer so we had to make the decision to put him to sleep. He went very peacefully, like the good boy he was, but we felt it was so unfair on him. He hadn't had a great life until he was four-years-old and we only got to have six years with him. We felt like he deserved more.

It wasn't until Buster died at the grand age of fifteen that I came across Jackie's website. We were again devastated when Buster died and I wanted to know that he was ok. It's something I never thought of doing when Frank died as I didn't really know anything about psychics then. During that reading Buster showed Jackie a picture of Frank, I was so amazed as I hadn't even mentioned Frank to Jackie. So a few weeks later I arranged another reading with Jackie to contact Frank.

Jackie began the reading by saying that she was speaking to Frank and felt that he was a gentle soul who had come out of his shell and that she thought he was a rescue – all correct! Now back to the point, I mentioned earlier about how we came to choose Frank, as he told Jackie that he was a 'sudden thought'. In a way that is true, as we decided on Buster and then took Frank as well, but it was one of

109

the best decisions we ever made. Frank said that he wasn't really interested in toys and he showed Jackie a rather desolate picture of his time before he came to live with us. He was shut outside in a yard, he wasn't abused but more neglected which explains why he was so sad when he came to us.

Frank then mentioned his illness, that it came out of the blue and by the time he showed symptoms it was too late. Even though I kind of knew what to expect from my previous reading with Jackie I was still amazed at the accuracy. Jackie told me she felt he had to be put to sleep but Frank told her he understood the decision as he wasn't going to get any better.

Frank relayed happy times of bouncing around with another dog. That was with Buster, they would be desperate to get off the lead and then would charge off at top speed, play fighting and often knocking each other over! Frank told Jackie that he also loved the car and going on journeys. He mentioned sitting on the sofa with me stroking his head and talking to him – we used to call him ' heavy head', as once he put his head on you he would drop off to sleep and you were pinned down! He also mentioned a hearth and liking to lie in front of the fire. This was also true and both dogs liked lying there. One day, when my mum had popped out, my dad had gone to light the fire and couldn't get up again. Mum found him lying in front of the hearth with both dogs lying across him with their heads nearly in the fire!

Frank said that he liked to know what was going on. That was almost an understatement! He would follow you around and anything new was a point of interest, so much so that another one of our nicknames for him was 'Inspector'! He could literally spend hours

Real Animal Communication Stories No.7

sniffing and inspecting anything new that came into the house. He wasn't allowed upstairs but would constantly try to sneak up just to see what he was missing, I would often see his cheeky face peeping around the corridor at the top of the stairs.

I knew from my previous reading with Jackie that not everything would maybe make sense at the time, so I made sure to write everything down in case it became apparent later. Frank mentioned my mum and then was showing Jackie a picture of a small beige dog. This dog was definitely connected to my mum. I thought it must be one of the Yorkshire Terriers we had while growing up as both were attached to my mum. However Jackie said she actually thought it was more like a strong built dog, a Corgi may be? Well I was really puzzled as Mum's dog when she was growing up was a poodle, I just couldn't place a Corgi but Jackie was certain that was more like the picture she was being given. I told Jackie that I would ask my mum.

When I phoned my mum that evening I relayed the details of the call with Jackie and mum was amazed at how accurate everything was. I casually glossed over the talk about a Corgi as fully expected Mum to say she knew nothing about that dog either. I was so convinced about what she would say that I only half heard her when she said that she did know a Corgi. I was already moving onto something else and had to ask her to repeat what she had just said! Mum told me that when she first moved into our house there was a Corgi there called Toby who belonged to my half-sister. Well I was absolutely stunned and so was mum! Toby had to have died over 40 years ago, I didn't even know about him! So well done Frank and well done Jackie – truly amazing!

I emailed Jackie straightaway to tell her and we both agreed that Frank would be really pleased with himself for knowing this and would be prancing around and doing a happy dance!

A sweet thing he mentioned was about watching the hedgehogs. Last year, for the first time in many years, hedgehogs appeared in our garden much to the interest of the 'Inspector'. I do hope they come back as they will bring such joy seeing them, especially with their added significance. I know Frank will be also watching too.

The readings with Jackie gave all of the family great comfort after the death of Buster and such happy memories and laughs about Frank. I would highly recommend Jackie's work and my only regret is not doing this when our dogs were still alive, but as Jackie says, 'Timing is timing'.

*****

Her most special pony in the world...

Holly and her pony Jimmy

Like many young girls, my childhood dream was to have my own pony. Sadly this was not to be but, fast-forward to me as a 38 year old, married mother of six-year-old twins and that wish was finally about to come true.

Jimmy definitely found us, rather than the other way around. My husband and I were both delighted that our children shared our own love of horses and encouraged them no end. They started riding at four-years-old but we were definitely not looking for a pony for them. They had recently been learning at a little riding school but we were informed that sadly, it was due to close. There was a pony called Jimmy

Real Animal Communication Stories No.7

there who had only been there a short time and was on loan from his previous home where he had been a companion pony. Recognising this was a waste of a bright, fit pony, his owner was happy for him to be sold to the right home. The instructor mentioned it to us and before I knew it we had this gorgeous, slightly scruffy, little Exmoor pony.

The plan was that he would live down the road in a neighbour's field, however, within two weeks I was head over heels in love with him and he was in our garden. Our grand plans of a landscaped garden were a thing of the past and the main focus was trying to teach Jimmy not to eat the flowers. He was far too bright for his own good sometimes – he knew exactly what he was and wasn't allowed to munch on but he also knew the best way to get some attention was to devour my wisteria. I was guaranteed to be with him in seconds!

Jimmy's new living arrangements also brought about some unexpected challenges... All was well until 6am every morning at precisely this time, he would come down onto the patio and stand under our bedroom window, where he would proceed to neigh his little head off until I popped my head out to say good morning! If the kitchen doors were left open he would see this as an invitation to come in for a wander around and likewise with the fitness room. We had many exercise classes with Jimmy half in the room and others with him actually in the room doing stretches in front of the mirror. For those of you who think I am crazy, I really do have photographic evidence!

I haven't mentioned that we did try using electric fencing, several times and in several ways, but this never put Jimmy off; there was always a way under, over or through it for Jimmy. Eventually, enough was enough and my husband put up a very sturdy wooden fence giving Jimmy a sizeable paddock with a much-needed boundary. Next came the stable with rubber matting and an enormous bed of shavings which Jimmy took to like a king to a throne.

The children loved riding him whenever they could and on days they were at school, I would take Jimmy running with the dogs and me. I am still not sure who enjoyed it more, him or the neighbours – they were quite astonished, but it kept both of us fit and was such a delightful time. If I ever stopped to talk to anyone for too long, Jimmy would let me know that he was bored by lifting his front leg and quite literally nudging my leg with his hoof. I imagine he picked this up by watching my children's attempts at getting my attention! Initially I had worried that Jimmy might be lonely without another equine friend but it soon became clear these fears were unfounded. There was no doubt that he was a happy boy and now saw me as his herd.

Not only did Jimmy become a great love of my life, but my pride and joy too. Long gone were the many scabs that he arrived with, his coat was so shiny I could check my lipstick in it and he was now at his ideal weight. I worked tirelessly in those cold dark winter months, drying his legs to keep his mud fever at bay. I fed him the best supplements I could find to make him as healthy as he could possibly be. He had an array of rugs for every eventuality and enough lotions and potions to rival my own collection. When we got Jimmy we were advised that he had suffered with Laminitis (a very painful condition of their hooves) so I religiously checked his feet for heat and pulses, we gave him minimal grass, soaked his hay

Real Animal Communication Stories No.7

and followed every recommended precaution I could find during my extensive, some would say obsessive, research.

However, despite our very best efforts, the dreaded laminitis struck one bitter January morning. It was the most awful experience to see my beautiful boy in such pain. I immediately called the vet who came with a supply of painkiller sachets and told me to put his feet in buckets of cold water for 15 minutes each, four times a day. No mean feat but if there was a chance it would help then I would absolutely convince Jimmy to do it. I sat with him hour after hour, day after day. I talked to him, I sang (very badly) to him, I cried and I laughed when he licked my face until he recovered. He was tested for Cushing's disease as that can be linked to the onset of laminitis but it came back negative so we were none the wiser. In March, I once more felt the initial warning signs in his feet but this time when I called my vet he told me told me three times I was probably imagining it and to just keep an eye on him. I quickly realised this vet was not to be trusted and went through two more vets until I found the lovely Lucy. Finally, I had a wonderful vet I trusted wholeheartedly and knew she was on our side.

We nursed him through this attack and the next, while testing for anything and everything that could be causing it. He was as good as gold as his feet were X-rayed and his plastic support shoes were fitted. Every test continued to come back clear but eventually we decided to treat him for Cushing's because he had all the symptoms apart from a positive blood test. He responded well to the medication almost immediately and we were so hopeful we had found the answer.

Even when Jimmy was poorly he kept his spark and would call me (very loudly!), every hour if I hadn't been to see him with a cup of mint tea or a cuddle. I frequently ended up with hay in my cup as he shared my drink so I decided the best option was to make him his own bowl of fresh mint tea whenever I made my own. He loved this and when he finished he would curl his big lips up in the air and make funny sounds. He enjoyed showing off and my laughter would only make him worse. He definitely became a high maintenance pony but it didn't bother me in the slightest because I enjoyed every minute I spent with him. Even when he called at 6am on freezing cold mornings I wouldn't allow anyone else to give him his breakfast. My husband was frequently envious of the attention Jimmy received and although I haven't admitted it before, I really do understand why!

One September afternoon, I left Jimmy happily playing with his ball at 5pm but when I went back to give him his supper at 6pm he was in such a bad way. He could hardly move and his legs were shaking in pain. I called Lucy who came immediately to our rescue. We were able to relieve his pain but needed to do X-rays the following morning to find out what was going on. Jimmy had never gone down so quickly before or behaved in the way he was. He was holding his left foot in the air and his legs were still shaking. Even in this pain he kept resting his head against my body and licking me. By the time we did X-rays in the morning I think Jimmy and I knew it wouldn't be good but to actually see the rotation of his pedal bone was still a shock. (When a horse/pony get laminitis inside the hoof can weaken as the laminae, which are like flanges that hold things together in the foot, get so weak that the main foot bone inside the foot, the pedal bone, can turn and sink down.)

The devastating decision to allow him to go to the 'Rainbow Bridge' was made and before I said my final heart-breaking goodbyes, I ran to the apple tree and returned to him laden with his favourite but forbidden treat. He feasted on the apples and covered me in sweet apple juice as I cried uncontrollably whist covering him in kisses. I feel somewhat ashamed to admit I didn't stay with him until the very end but I was in a mess and also didn't want to distress him further. I left him in the strong and loving arms of my husband and the vet. They assure me he went quickly and peacefully with an apple in his mouth.

My grief surprised even me. I was quite literally heartbroken and felt like I had lost my best friend. The feeling of loss and desperation was overwhelming and it was at this time I read about Jackie. I have had numerous personal readings in the past, a number of which have been nothing short of amazing, but never with animals. However, I didn't waste any time and quickly contacted Jackie. She responded the same day and I had a reading booked for about ten days time. Before the call, I had to send Jackie a picture of Jimmy and a couple of details such as his name and age.

As the time for the call approached I became quite nervous but Jackie's warm and friendly manner settled me immediately. I was delighted to hear she had made contact with Jimmy and he was there with her. The very first thing Jackie told me about was the reason for Jimmy's passing. She was shockingly accurate, right down to the detail of him holding his front foot in the air and this set the tone for the whole reading. Jimmy asked Jackie to reassure me it was the right time and confirmed that we had both known it that morning, even before the X-rays were taken. She described my unusual and wonderful relationship with Jimmy perfectly and he explained how he had been sent to me because he needed extra care at that time. Jackie went on to tell me, so accurately, about Jimmy's life before he came to us. Amusingly, he described himself as a big pet teddy bear in our family and how much he loved it. He showed Jackie our dogs and children and even went on to describe Stanley, a dog that stays with us for his holidays. Stanley had seriously upset Jimmy in the early days but after a very close call with Jimmy's feet and Stanley's head, Stanley began to respect Jimmy and they became friends. He described his time and relationship with us as very special and unique, which is so true.

When Jackie recounted the actual words I kept repeating to Jimmy on the final morning I found myself covered in goose bumps but I smiled as Jackie tried to understand what Jimmy was telling her when he showed her an image of me with a cup of tea. She said he was saying something like, "Come on, I'm ready for it." My boy was describing how he used to ask for the end of my morning cuppa hence getting his own fresh mint tea! He was proud to tell Jackie how smart he always looked when he was with us. Anyone that met Jimmy knows just how true that is.

I used to love lifting Jimmy's forelock and kissing the soft hair beneath it. I kept telling my husband how much I was missing that and during the reading Jimmy told Jackie the same thing. He asked Jackie to tell me that what we had was incredible and that we had given each other something very special. He had

Real Animal Communication Stories No.7

left a light in my heart and wanted me to smile with the memories. He described to Jackie where he was and how he wanted me to remember him – imagine him on a hill of lush green grass, looking down at me with the sun behind him. This all sounded lovely but because it wasn't recounting a specific event I didn't pay too much attention at the time. However, I must admit that it has really helped me since. A picture of my brave boy in this happy place has replaced some memories of that sad last day.

When Jimmy was with us I promised myself that I would never have another pony but very quickly I found an empty paddock too painful to look at. Not only had I lost my boy but I had lost my daily routine and I really wanted it back. I could never, ever replace Jimmy but I was now confident we could have fun with another pony. We had begun to look at ponies for sale and two weeks on we already had another Exmoor, Pegasus, due to arrive the following day. I was also very keen on getting a young Exmoor and was in the process of making plans to go and see two in Wales. However, I couldn't help but wonder how Jimmy would feel about another pony or ponies in his paddock and this reservation was making me a little uneasy about the new pony's imminent arrival. I hadn't told Jackie any of this but asked how Jimmy would feel about another pony. He very quickly said it absolutely wasn't a problem and that maybe we should get a pair of ponies!! I laughed and explained about the new one coming and going to see the others. The two ponies in Wales are brother and sister (Maggie May) so I asked if he had any thoughts on which one we should go for. He advised that the boy may be a little pushy and commented about Maggie May being linked to Rod Stewart – amazingly my dad had commented exactly the same a couple of nights before. Very kindly, Jimmy also assured me he would be around to help with the new ponies.

I found my reading with Jackie much more emotional than I imagined it to be but I think that was because of the accuracy and understanding from Jackie. Although emotional, I am so pleased I did it and absolutely wouldn't hesitate to do it again in the future. The end of the call left me with so much reassurance that we did the right thing and that Jimmy knew how loved he was and also that he had been so happy with his life. I even feel sure I will see him again in many years to come. My husband can be sceptical of my beliefs but even he was blown away by the reading and has found comfort in it. Jimmy was, after all, very much loved by the whole family.

We used to do a particular hack with Jimmy and as he became wiser and particularly when we went before his supper time, he would literally stop in the same place, half way down a field and turn around to go home. By then he was generally the boss and it made us laugh so we would just follow his lead and make our way home. On Pegasus's second day with us, we took her for her first hack and in exactly the same spot as Jimmy, she stopped, turned around and tried to go back home! She isn't the boss....yet, so we made her continue and we did the whole walk but we couldn't believe it. I am sure it was Jimmy's way of letting us know he was with us on the walk!

My bond with Jimmy was strong from the beginning but after what we had been through together it was bigger and stronger than I could ever have imagined possible. Jimmy taught me so much about love and trust between horse and human. As I begin to

Real Animal Communication Stories No.7

reluctantly accept that he has moved on, I know that ultimately I will look back on our time together and always remember how extremely fortunate I have been to experience such a bond and unconditional love from the most special pony in the world. He was my magical pony straight out of a fairy tale so it is perfect that he is remembered within the pages of a book.

*****

The chance to learn for both of us…

Chrissie and her dog Chance

I got my first dog when I was sixteen years old. I went and bought an Old English Sheepdog pup with money left to me by my Godmother who had sadly been killed in a road accident. I wanted something living to remember her by and I have never looked back. All my other dogs have always somehow found me, from being left in my garden to someone ringing at the right moment to say they knew about one needing a home. Every one of them has been special in its own way, but none as special as my Chance. I find myself for the first time in a long while, waiting for the next one to come into my life, if or when the time is right. We will know as soon as we look into each other's eyes if we are meant to be together or not.

I had lost my previous dog two weeks earlier and was not looking for another when I received a call from a breeder who was an acquaintance. She phoned to say that she had a ten-month-old bitch Golden Retriever returned to her, as the man who had bought her could not get on with the dog. Apparently she was too timid to do anything with and too dark to breed from as the demand was for pale coloured retrievers. I went along to see her and saw two of the largest, saddest brown eyes looking out at me from the back of a kennel and I knew then and there she was coming home with me. That was to be the best decision of my life. I called her Chance after the Abba song – *Take a Chance on Me.*

Life was not easy for the first six months. She had obviously been harshly treated and was incredibly nervous which just created a vicious circle for her. However throughout all this she was just so desperate to please and to be loved, and give love too. Over time, and with lots of love and fun, Chance eventually relaxed and simply took life as she found it.

When she was three years old I found a small lump on her, which turned out to be an aggressive cancer. I had it removed and then the next one appeared a couple of years later, then more frequently. Her last lump was removed in October 2015 when I commented to my vet at the time, if these are showing on the outside what is happening on the inside? He responded that we will deal with that when it happens. Little did I know then that within four months, at the age of nine, this would be exactly what would happen and what a huge void she would leave in my life.

Going back to the beginning of our life journey together when I collected her from the breeder... No sooner had I driven half a mile from the kennel, she started to hyperventilate and was violently sick in the car. She cowered in the back waiting to be punished and looked confused at my gentle words of encouragement and soothing. As we got home she slithered out, waiting to be hit, and again was confused when I simply took the rug out and just

Real Animal Communication Stories No.7

dealt with it. She nervously came into the kitchen but would not venture beyond the doorway into the lounge as this had obviously been no go territory in the past. I introduced her to the outside of her new home and the open fields where she stuck by my side like glue. I settled her down for the night and woke up the next morning to find my leather coat had been eaten, well part of it had! Her taste then moved to lino and later she tried to dig her way through the cement floor! I then decided to have the floor of the cottage changed to flag stones and put in pheromone diffusers to try and help calm her.

She spent the first six months with me crawling on her belly, always looking to be chastised whenever she was called. However, her confidence was slowly growing all the time as she eventually started to learn to trust and let herself love and be loved. She learnt to venture out of the kitchen and even found her way upstairs. We were growing together. She had anxiety issues to begin with and decided one day, when I was out, to fly unaided from the bedroom window. I returned to no dog to greet me. I ran round checking every room for her, noticed the ornaments from the window ledge in the bedroom on the floor and saw that the top quarter window was ajar. My heart sank. I went outside and started calling frantically for her. I spotted her bouncing up the drive, tail wagging, and looking really pleased with herself with my neighbour in tow. She had jumped out of a bedroom window and must have bounced off the table below and got away without a single injury from her adventure. Phew!

She also learnt to play as next door to me, they had a Dalmatian called Horace about the same age, who was a re-home as well. They became great friends and always called for each other to go and play in the field. They chased each other round and round, playing tag, and Chance developed the art of mastering the high dive forward roll at speed, and standing on her head (much to Horace's displeasure who, as a gangly teenager had no flexibility or balance. Introduced into this mix were a dozen Shetland ponies, a Highland pony and chickens but Chance's favourite time was watching interactive 'cat TV' next door. She would spend hours shadowing the cat's every movement. When the cat stopped she stopped, when the cat turned to look at her she looked the opposite way over her shoulder. The first time the cat brushed up against her she trembled in anticipation and nearly wet herself. Cat TV was only surpassed when Basil the rabbit arrived on the scene. Every time Chance went out through the gate she had to go and see Basil who was just as daft with her as she was with him.

Chance was becoming the perfect companion. My friends swore she was human and could speak just through the looks she gave us. We were both becoming well trained.

I had a riding accident and broke my neck which changed things for us. During my recovery time Chance was my constant companion; she instinctively read my moods and slotted in beside me, making me laugh and keeping me going, or just lying quietly with me. As a result of the accident we had to sell our small holding as there was uncertainty about my degree of recovery. We moved and from day one, Chance just adapted to our new way of life – it was as if we had always lived there. I have never met a dog with such a huge heart and generous personality. She soon became 'friends' with other people and dogs in the area. People always commented on what

Real Animal Communication Stories No.7

a fantastic, well behaved dog she was. An old farmer summed it up one day when she sat waiting patiently for me whilst I was chatting to him. He simply said, "That's a happy dog who absolutely loves and adores you," to which I replied "and me her." She became affectionately known as 'velcro dog' as she always stuck to me.

Fortunately I made a good recovery and we walked miles together down by the river, along bridle paths and country lanes. She continued to perfect her sequence of rolls and balances much to the amusement of everyone who saw her in action. She loved the snow and would roll around forever in it. In fact, we have been known to do sneaky 'snow angels' together in the really deep snow and play fetch the snowball. Every patch of grass she passed needed to be rolled on.

Chance has also had the job of role model for many a young pup, from Jack Russell to Bernese Mountain dog and everything in-between. She showed them how to come when called and not run off and was a regular training companion.

Her greeting was second to none – as a retriever she always had to bring one of her favourite soft toys to you as you opened the door. If dry, she would run outside, lie on her back and juggle the said toy in the air with her paws and if wet, the routine took place in the lounge.

I worked from home so during the day she would be with me in the office and at night we would have our snuggle time on the settee together.

Chance was suddenly taken ill one day just before I was due to fly to Australia for a month. I rushed her to the emergency vet and they found nothing obviously wrong. I took her to my vet the next day who gave her a couple of injections and she was back up and running as good as new again. I thought about cancelling the trip but as she was back to her bouncy self I went, leaving her at my friends with their two dogs, which is where she always went if I was away with work. It was a second home for her. A couple of days before I was due back she went off her food. I got a home coming second to none from her, but within 24 hours she was back at the vets and went rapidly downhill. She spent a couple of days at the vet hospital before I was allowed to see her. When I did, I knew unless they had some fairy dust in the top drawer that she needed to come home right then. We had the night together on the settee and the results came back the next morning saying that the aggressive cancer had distorted her small intestine and there was nothing that could be done. There were tears and cuddles and we thanked each other for all the laughter and love we had shared on the way and said our goodbyes, and she died in my arms on the settee at home. It was the last kind act I could do for her. I swear she had waited for me to come home to be there with her at the end. So many people were upset by the loss of Chance. She was so loved and still is loved by so many.

Over the weeks I felt guilty that I had gone away, I missed her so much and swore that some nights she came up on the bed with me as she had always done. A friend mentioned Jackie Weaver and said that she did dog readings. In my teens I had developed my psychic ability but had been scared of it so walked away. I knew that it was possible to connect with people who had passed over, so maybe animals would be possible too.

Real Animal Communication Stories No.7

My reading with Jackie was amazingly accurate; she covered so much of what was mentioned above. Chance said she had a 'malaise' all her life and that it did not matter if I had been away or not, her body just could not cope anymore. She was a good girl with a huge personality and sense of fun. She said people and dogs loved her and that she accepted her lot and did not complain – that was so true, as in spite of all her treatments and operations, she stayed the sunny personality she always was.

She said that she had to come to see me at night as I was so broken hearted but one day I would be happy and content, just as she was now, in spirit. She mentioned to Jackie that I had psychic ability. This I confirmed and said that I had had that said to me just a few weeks ago too! In my teens I had developed my psychic ability but had been scared of it so walked away. Jackie said there was absolutely nothing to fear; this gift is so natural and can help living animals as well as owners grieving for their passed over animals. This I can vouch for, as this reading really set my heart at peace as it was so definitely Chance talking. Jackie spoke of other dogs, especially one who was not well, and other memories personal to us. Chance then volunteered that she wanted to work with me and be my guide for the readings. I got such comfort in knowing that she was okay and by taking this new path of animal communication, I knew that we would become a dynamic duo again. Jackie described her as an Angel on Earth, which is so true as she touched so many lives and hearts.

As I said, I had developed my psychic ability previously and now I really felt like the time was right to get back in tune. I had a personal reading myself a few weeks before which basically saw me working with animals in a healing capacity of some sort. The jigsaw was starting to take shape. This was the third time I had been told about my own psychic powers so I asked Jackie if she could teach me how to read for animals. She said absolutely and that if animals say you are psychic, they are rarely wrong. So, there and then I booked an appointment for a few weeks time to do a lesson via Webcam on Skype.

When I did my communication lesson with Jackie, she taught me in a very clear and simple way. This was a relief as I have read some articles that seem so very complicated and not just straightforward telepathy, which Jackie explains it as. She taught me to understand how to get and interpret the information and how to get past our logical brain. The 'logical brain' issue is the thing that all people learning to do any form of psychic work have the main problem with – me included. Having now been shown various techniques by Jackie, I was amazed at how much I could pick up just by linking in via a photo of her own living Collie dog, Sally. I too just had the basic information like Jackie asks for such as: name, age, gender and how long the owner had had them. I found Sally could give me information about areas of her former or existing ailments, favourite toys and walks, other pets, her characteristics, how she got on or not with other dogs, her loves and sadness. By the end of the reading I felt I really knew Jackie's Sally in person! My feelings, having done this (with the help of my lovely Chance I am sure) were indescribable and I know I will go on to do more.

All this has helped confirm what was already in my head – I had come to a cross roads and I have now made my decision on which path to take. As well as

Real Animal Communication Stories No.7

practicing my animal readings I have started Reiki with the intention of developing that with animals as well. Chance said, "I am a lesson to you all." Such a poignant statement, and so very true; we taught each other so much and it looks like we are going to carry on teaching each other into the future. Me and my Chance together again.

*****

A simply adorable and fun girl...

Debbie and her dog Freddie

Freddie came into my life in 2003 and bravely departed in 2015. She was twelve years old. I had waited many years until the time was right to have my own puppy and I could be at home to enjoy and devote lots of time to my canine companion. Some people thought it strange that I named her Freddie but it suited her, it was short for Frederica but she was always Freddie.

Freddie was one of the six Jack Russell pups born to caring parents who were friendly and excellent role models. All of the pups were gorgeous but Freddie stood out because she was a very pretty tri-coloured girl with attitude. She fitted into the palm of my hand and looked at me calmly in a 'Take me or leave me' manner. That was that – she was the one!

Once home, Freddie tottered into the lounge, peed on the carpet and looked at me as if to say 'What about it?' I wanted her to have the run of the house and not be confined although this did prove to be somewhat of a challenge at times; she loved to chew things such as telephone wires, and whatever took her fancy. She never went for the usual shoes or socks, but had an appetite for cables and her favourite activity was chewing the plastic links at the bottom of the window

129

blinds in the lounge until they were completely destroyed. She loved balls and squeaky furry toys and destroyed many of these with great gusto. She had toys that were bigger than her and she happily dragged them along but the mission was always to remove the squeak from inside.

Freddie had the sweetest nature. She was loving, fun, playful, naughty, cuddly, curious, intelligent, loyal, brave, determined and absolutely spoilt! She pretty much ruled the roost but knew the boundaries even if she often chose to ignore them. She rarely barked and it was usually when whoever was at the door was already in the house! Freddie was wonderful, easy company (when it suited her) and loved to sit on the front doorstep watching the world go by.

My partner fell in love with her at first sight and they were very good friends. She adored us as we did her. Wherever we went, people, young and old often stopped to admire and chat to her. She could be aloof and a little dismissive of their compliments if she was busy. She liked other dogs but liked to be respected. As she got older she did not appreciate being jumped on or knocked over. She loved nothing more than snoozing in her bed with us in the room talking quietly. She disliked noise and would exit the room if you put a DVD on and give you 'the look'. She had sleeping areas all over the house and would always seek out any sunshine. I sometimes found her draped over the top of the settee in a bid to grab the last rays.

Freddie had a huge personality and we miss her every day. She spent most of her time with me and I took her on trips whenever possible as she loved the adventure. Even a trip to the local shop in the car was cause for great excitement. She liked to sit in the

Real Animal Communication Stories No.7

front seat and if I had a passenger then she would look at them as if to say, "why are you in my seat?"

Freddie had her health problems over the years but she was always strong, brave and quickly recovered. In early 2015 she started to go downhill quickly and was later diagnosed with dementia. It was obvious that this was not normal ageing and it was heart-breaking to see her decline. She had the best veterinary treatment and was also under the care of a homeopathic vet who helped her enormously. Sadly it became clear that life was becoming a huge struggle for her and she was no longer enjoying all the things she loved doing such as going out in the car, walks and playing etc. She was still eating well but struggling to drink and this caused her to become dehydrated. Towards the end, I was sleeping downstairs with her as she would pace for most of the night and get confused. It was hard, and exhausting too.

We knew that Freddie was no longer enjoying life and when she communicated clearly to us both that she was ready, she was put to sleep at home by a calm and compassionate vet in November 2015. Her transition was dignified and peaceful and I know she was grateful. She had the best life and the best death we could give her.

A few months later, I decided to contact an animal communicator. I missed Freddie dreadfully and was grieving but I did not feel guilty at her passing as I believed that is what she had wanted and that she was in a happier place. My partner was really struggling and could not get over the fact that Freddie had yelped at one point during the euthanasia – he felt tortured. I am not religious but I believe in the

Universe and energy and trust that I will be reunited with Freddie later on.

I did some research on the Internet and came across Jackie's website. I had been let down by another animal communicator and I was eager to get on with this. I found Jackie to be professional and efficient. She got back to me promptly and I had an appointment quickly planned.

I have an open mind and was looking forward to our telephone communication and to be able to offer my partner the reassurance that Freddie was well and happy in spirit. Jackie called at the designated time and I liked her upbeat, down to earth manner. She described Freddie as she was: an individual, easy going, amenable, a happy little soul – all so true. Jackie said Freddie was very sprightly, well behaved, determined and aware of everything. Freddie described herself as 'simply adorable' which would be my words too. She said that Freddie was often behind me, or seeking out my company, but not in a needy way. Freddie said that she loved to go out with us but also knew very well when she was going to be left at home. This was so true, and boy, she would make us feel so guilty just by staying in her bed and looking at you, with 'that look'.

She said that she loved to be on my lap for cuddles. She declared she was also a Daddy's girl but gave her love in equal shares. She was a blessed little being, and indeed she was. Freddie communicated her sheer joy of life and how she loved her walks and trips in the car, saying that she would never run off which is correct. Oh how Freddie made me smile when Jackie repeated her line that said, 'There are sheep up here but I don't chase them'. This made such sense as she was not a chaser and would always

Real Animal Communication Stories No.7

stay close and how lovely to know she can see sheep in this special place. Jackie said that she was showing her lots of tall trees (she loved the woods) and her delight of being in her garden – a real nature lover. She said she liked other dogs and was not into fighting. True, she might have been a terrier with her own mind but she was a gentle girl.

Freddie knew that she was comfortable and spoilt and had a better life than a lot of animals. She stated, 'You would go a long way to find a dog like me.' That made me laugh and I agreed. I always felt that she was a wise little soul and teacher and the communication confirmed this.

Jackie felt that Freddie's decline was quite rapid and that she was disorientated. Freddie was aware of everything and knew we had helped her to transition. She felt that she had lost the battle and was ready to leave and was now her true self again. She clarified it by saying, "I know I went — but it doesn't change me." I felt happy that we had correctly interpreted her needs.

I said to Jackie about my partner's continued struggle re: her yelp. Freddie confirmed that at her transition she yelped but that it was not due to pain, just a reaction and it was all over quickly. I said I would tell my partner who is Italian, and in response, Freddie stated, 'Typical Italian to hold onto things; he will get over it!' She always did have a keen sense of humour and would often make us laugh. Freddie remembered me stroking her ears after she had the sedative injection and she recalled feeling woozy. She remembered feeling peaceful and having a blanket laid over her to cover her shoulders with her head uncovered – amazing details.

Also, in relation to my partner, Jackie was saying 'Bella' and asking 'Is this a name'? Having an Italian partner, I said that in Italian, Bella means beautiful. He later told me he did call Freddie 'Bella' sometimes.

Freddie answered my questions in detail and let me know her wishes and how she would like to be remembered. She wants her ashes to be scattered: Some on the front lawn slope in the garden, some in the woods and she requested an apple tree be planted to bear fruit, so to put some there too! No pressure then! She also asked that I give a framed picture of her to my partner and said, "He may cry but it will help him." Lastly, Freddie knew I had a snow globe that I keep in my bedroom, and she said to occasionally shake it just for fun. She gave me permission to give some of her toys, beds, blankets etc., to charity stating, "I am not precious, there are others in need".

She also told me that she is never far away. I do often feel that she is with me, especially when I am in the car. I asked Freddie is she was aware of the Reiki healing I often gave her and she said, 'Yes, and not only when I was not well. I can help with healing if you ask – I believe in it." I thought that was lovely. I also asked who was looking after her in spirit and she stated firmly, "I can look after myself, I am capable." She did however relent and added that Mabel was with her. Mabel was an old friend of mine who died many years ago and we were very close. She was a kind person and so I now know Freddie is in safe hands.

There was a lot of detail in the communication and I found it accurate. It is emotional to pen this story and I am shedding tears as I write but I am pleased that

Freddie's character and love of life came through strongly. I knew it was her as Jackie could not have known all the detail. I thank Jackie, and her dearly departed cat Stan, for their help. I found it very interesting and comforting. Jackie is a skilled communicator.

Freddie thinks that I should have another dog later on and that it should be a boy and not like her. She thought a dark dog and a whippet type would suit and would like it to be a rescue dog. She added, "Spirit knows best." Wow.

Lastly, I will share these words from Freddie, which we thought were so beautiful... "I was gold dust in a dog." She most certainly was. Ciao Bella.

*****

A boy not to be ignored...

Kate and Paul's cat Oscar

My partner Paul and myself are great animal lovers, but never planned to have a cat! However, eight years ago our lives were totally changed when a little ginger boy cat came trotting over to say, 'Hello'. His tag told me he was called Oscar, and he lived just round the corner from our house.

Day after day he would come over for attention but we tried not to encourage him so never fed him and time and time again we would return him to his owner. It turned out she had another two Burmese cats, neither related to Oscar. Eventually we came to the conclusion that maybe Oscar would prefer to be an only cat, so we talked this through with his owner. She decided that for his sake we should take Oscar on permanently. I have to say, I am sure Oscar had already decided this outcome weeks before we did!

And so in he moved, and immediately started bossing us around!

He was very much a lap cat, and always shared his affections with both of us. He could be very vocal and also snored a lot! He liked to get up at 3.00am and if you ignored him, our bedside table would be swiftly cleared of its book, lamp and clock! He was kind, gentle and fearless, which did give us cause to worry... When he was out, he loved nothing better than to spot an open door or window in a house, car or garage, and he loved visiting the neighbours! In fact, he became loved by others and would receive his own Christmas cards!

In May 2016, Oscar developed a reverse sneeze, which our lovely vet hoped would be either a head cold or polyps, and put him on a two-week course of antibiotics. These seemed to help and Oscar carried on eating and drinking as usual but, just as the two weeks was ending, his breathing became noisy and he didn't want his food.

So first thing Monday morning we took him to the vet. He took him in and said he would give our boy a general anaesthetic so he could have X-rays and blood tests. At 3.00pm we had a call from him to say Oscar was having trouble coming round and was unable to breathe for himself. He said to please get there as soon as possible. We dropped everything and went straight to the surgery. When we arrived, we found our little man laid out flat on a blanket, tube in his mouth and a nurse pumping air for him. It was obvious we had no choice but to allow our vet to gently give Oscar his final injection, and within seconds he passed away. The nurse gently curled Oscar into his sleeping position whilst our tears flowed and our hearts broke.

Real Animal Communication Stories No.7

Our vet explained the X-rays showed a large hard lump behind, and also joined, to Oscars soft palate. This was in an inoperable place and would very likely be cancerous. Our vet was fantastic throughout, and was so kind to me when I returned a couple of days later with more questions, full of grief and worrying of did we do the right thing?

Our grief was immense, and I needed to know if Oscar blamed us, so I Googled 'Animal Psychic' and found the name Jackie Weaver. Although I had not heard of her before, I knew she and her cat Stan were the right pair to help us. I immediately sent for her book, *The Voice Of Spirit Animals*, and watched an interview with her on YouTube.

I sent Jackie an email asking her if she could help me. She replied the same day bless her, advising me to wait a couple of weeks for Oscar to settle in to spirit, and for me to be a bit stronger emotionally. True to her word, Jackie called me June 1st at 8.00pm, and her lovely voice instantly made me feel calm and gave me faith. Oscar started telling Jackie how he was a gentle cat, very 'doggified', and would come if you called his name – that was our boy! He told her about his cancer being in an inoperable place and affecting his breathing, and he could tell it had spread to other places. He said he had a very dignified death and that he had been cremated and was now back with us. He had been very loved, and received and given pure happiness.

I spent a lot of time during the phone call laughing, as he went on to tell Jackie so many funny incidents and things that only myself and Paul knew about, and were so accurate! I asked through Jackie, had he meant to leave home when he was missing for four days? He replied, "I got a lift, by accident!" He confirmed what we felt had probably happened, and as I said earlier, he loved to get into people's cars. Jackie thought his ride was in the back of a van and that he had then had to make his own way back.

After the reading I felt enormous peace, and in a strange way, happiness. I had gone from anxiety and real despair to a very calm state, knowing Oscar didn't blame us for letting him go. I have always wanted to believe in the spirit world, and after finding Jackie, I have no doubts that there is something more, and that all our beloved animals go there and party. I know that we will be with them again one day, with no pain, just pure contentment. We will both continue to talk in our heads and out loud to our boy, and I know although he is not here in body for us to stroke, he is here in spirit, and in our hearts and souls always. He is still our truly beloved and best friend forever. Thank you Oscar for choosing us – you have changed our lives beyond words and introduced us to the wonderful world of the spiritual realms.

And as time rolled on…

We thought our story was at an end as we were both determined we wouldn't have another cat but, the house felt so empty and no longer a home. So five months down the line, we found ourselves looking at cats and kittens for sale. We decided we would like our next cat to be an oriental, and Paul was keen to have a Havana boy. Havana cats are sleek and have the most amazing eyes. After some research, we found a breeder who we were happy to purchase a kitten from, a friendly and helpful lady, nothing was too much trouble for her. She said she might have

Real Animal Communication Stories No.7

some Havanas later in the month, but she did have a very new litter with a black boy if we were interested.

I felt so confused, really guilty about having another. I was worried about how Oscar would feel, so I emailed Jackie to ask her and didn't mention any specific cats or kittens. That same evening I received an amazing reply from her. She started off by saying that whatever animal *is* to come to you, *will*! She said that Oscar wouldn't wish me to feel guilty as animals are not selfish like that. Jackie ended her email with these exact words... 'I see a small/fine black cat with striking eyes?!' As soon as I showed Paul he knew what to do! Never mind waiting for a Havana, he reserved the little black boy in the litter, as Paul says he must be the cat Jackie had seen! It is very early days as our boy is only a week old, but he already has his name as Paul has chosen to call him Henry.

Jackie has helped us so much through the past five months, with her spot on reading with Oscar and her vision and description of Henry. The comfort and love she has sent in her emails answering questions and fears from myself have been invaluable. She is truly a remarkable lady who I thank God I found.

*****

A real Angel on Earth...

Anne and her dog Emma

In 2015 we moved back to the UK from Australia. We are in our sixties and had been out there for eleven years and five in Asia before that. We thought life was settled there, but we had such a dreadful time and, after a visit home to the UK two years ago, we returned to Australia knowing that we had to come home. When we got back to Tasmania we started the

139

procedure of selling the house and all that it involved. It took a year and a lot of upset.

We had our two dogs, Emma the most beautiful Golden Retriever and Mr. Darcey a very handsome black and white Cocker Spaniel. (We had lost our old Spaniel who we had rescued from the RSPCA and Emma pined desperately for him, so we found Mr Darcey. It was love at first sight and they adored each other.) We loved them so much.

Towards the nearing of the house completion Emma, only aged six, became very ill, and eventually passed away in October 2015. Our hearts were broken to say the least. Mr Darcey was very lost without her. When the people came to buy our house, they had a family and a fabulous dog too. Everyone fell in love with Mr Darcey and amazingly, they asked if we would like him to stay in Tasmania in the house and become their family dog too. As hard as this was to even contemplate, it seemed as if a solution was being offered to help us all: We were worried about the long flight for him (complete with three changes), quarantine and the uncertainty of where we would end up living in the UK and here was his dream come true... a new friend to run and play with and a family with children who we were sure would adore him and keep him safe. With heavy hearts, we agreed and knew it was the right thing to do.

In July 2016 my husband and I decided to attend *The Healing Weekend* in Somerset. It is a huge holistic fair and this is where I met Jackie. I sat down and asked to have a reading to see if our beloved dog Emma would come through and talk to me. I needed to know she was okay and talk about what had happened. I hoped seeing Jackie would help ease the pain of it all... I walked away in tears, not in despair

Real Animal Communication Stories No.7

but in amazement and gratefulness to know she is still there for my husband and myself.

Jackie looked at Emma's photo on my husband's phone and asked her to come forward and connect with us. Jackie started by saying that Emma is giving her the sound noisy birds – they were so noisy, like they were parrots squawking. At this point Jackie did not know we had recently come home from Australia so she would not know that every morning we would have cockatoos land on the veranda for their morning seed. They would squawk and squawk until we went out with their breakfast!

She told me that Emma was a gentle soul and an Angel on Earth. Jackie explained that sometimes these very special animals, for whatever reason, seem to go to Heaven early. (Emma was only with us five years before she passed, so her passing was a complete shock.) Emma said how she loved: being brushed, loved leaning against you, having her head stroked and how she loved walking side by side with our other dog, Mr Darcey.

Jackie then started coughing and gasping as she couldn't get her breath for a short time and then asked if this would have been relevant as to why Emma passed over. I nodded and Jackie volunteered the word 'auto-immunity'. I explained, for some unknown reason, a couple of years previously, Emma had started leaking urine and the vets gave us tablets for this, but then two years later she started coughing, and the vet gave us tablets for this too. In the October it had got so bad we took her back, and we had to leave Emma with them. When we went back to see them, we were told that both sides of her throat had collapsed. They said this can happen but usually on just one side so they can stitch back the collapsed

141

throat!! It turned out that she had some form of an auto-immune disease and there was nothing we could do for her. She was going to have to be put to sleep as she was going to suffer terribly. So, we had to say goodbye to our Angel and it broke our hearts.

Emma wanted us to know that towards the end of her life it was not painful just difficult – Emma explained that she would lie down as she couldn't walk far, not through lack of immobility but her breathing. She would lie at our feet and we would talk to her and she would look at us and her tail would wag.

To try and ease our suffering Emma also made a valid point: that had we put her on a plane back here to the UK she probably would not have made it, and worse still had she died in transit she would not have had us both there like she did when she passed over at the vets. This way, she could go onto pastures new, and be with us forever in spirit wherever we were.

She told Jackie that she loved our new home here in England and that we had used bright colours in our renovations, and yes we have... As it was an old property we kept the walls white but we have: a turquoise settee a purple chair, a lime green footstool, and five wonderfully coloured lampshades over the kitchen work tops, of teal, purple, green, yellow and lime! So yes, bright colours we most certainly do have!

Jackie asked if we had steps outside our backdoor. I confirmed we did and Jackie said that Emma was saying to be careful and it seemed as if they were neither straight nor safe? Well, the house is an old 1400's half a barn and we have renovated it from its 1991 renovations. The previous owners had not put up any fencing/barriers round the steps outside which

Real Animal Communication Stories No.7

drop down 8ft as it is an upside down house! Outside there is a stone staircase which, I am guessing, used to be up to the barn where they stored hay or such like. The steps have worn away over centuries, and can get slippery in the rain and of course nothing to stop you slipping off the edge down an 8ft drop! Spot on Emma!

Jackie also said that I would be, or was involved in working for a charity. This is true and I am now working for the National Trust. Jackie said Emma was showing her a picture of me smelling a flower in my hand. Wow, yesterday as I did my shift, I walked through the garden and picked some lavender heads and crushed them in my hands and smelt the wonderful aroma. I did, I did!! How wonderful Emma was watching.

Jackie suddenly said she could see the most awesome, vibrant rainbow and did I know the significance of this? I did and explained that in Tasmania in the autumn and spring, it had the most wonderful rainbows. The climate there is warm in summer and cold in winter (yes, cold in Australia!) with snow on mountains and with the clear air when it rains and the mist rises from the Derwent Valley the rainbows are amazing. How funny that Emma, our beautiful Golden Retriever, remembers them and can relate the beauty back to me on this day.

I asked Jackie to ask Emma about Mr Darcey and she immediately said that he was bringing much joy and could see children. Emma said that we had done the best thing possible for him and he would have a companion of a little dog which he was used to having. Now how did Jackie know this? Although I knew from his new family he was happy, I thank God that Mr Darcey is truly happy and thank Emma for letting us know.

We miss them both so much it isn't true, but also knowing that Emma and Mr Darcey are so happy makes my heart jump with joy. Now it probably didn't look like I was jumping with joy when I left Jackie, because I couldn't stop the tears hurtling down my cheeks, it has been a painful and upsetting two years.

This, I hope, is the end of that pain knowing all is right with the world. I am grateful to Jackie and of course Emma, who Jackie described as an Angel on Earth; our beloved Emma who wasn't going to be here for long because of her beauty, kindness and ability to understand us humans so much. To know she still wants to be around us forever makes the unbearable more bearable and beautiful in its own way.

Thank you Jackie, Thank you Emma, this is maybe the day where I can move on at last.

*****

Postscript

Once again a huge thank you to all my lovely friends: Diane, Becci, Shirley, Andy, Moyra and all others who, as my pre-checkers and post-checkers, have helped this book come together. You are so wonderful and helpful and I am so grateful to you all.

To my guides Rolf and Stan, without you my life would not be what it is. Last but definitely not least, a huge thanks to each every one of you who trusted me to communicate with your animal and wrote your story for this book. It has been a joy to connect with them for you and I know people will have enjoyed reading about their stories.

If I have worked for you and you think people would like to read your story, then feel free to email me on info@animalpsychic.co.uk and we can go from there. Please don't worry if you have not written a story before, I hadn't until my first book! I can give you a bit of guidance and, as long as you write the gist of it, I can do the rest.

Bless you all and may you and your animals stay well and safe and do enjoy talking to them knowing that they do understand what you say!

If you want to be kept informed of what I am getting up to, TV appearances, what my next book is etc. I do send out the occasional newsletter. If you go on to my website and scroll down to the bottom of the first page, you will see a picture of my cat Buddy looking inquisitive and you can sign up from there. I promise, your email address is totally protected and never shared.

Thank you for choosing and reading my book and if you like what I do and want to read more, here are the other books that I have written too.

They are all available on Amazon in paperback and digital. If you don't mind me asking... but if you can spare a minute to write a review about this book (or other ones of mine that you have read) I would be most grateful. It is the public's opinion that helps others make their choice of reading material. So, if you feel this book would be informative, enjoyable or even enlightening to someone else, a few words would help guide them.

Real Animal Communication Stories No.7

Jackie Weaver
'The Animal Psychic'
www.animalpsychic.co.uk

Printed in Great Britain
by Amazon